HINDUISM AT A GLANCE

D1096890

By the same author

OUR EDUCATION (3rd ed)

RELIGION AND MODERN DOUBTS (3rd ed)

SRI RAMAKRISHNA AND SPIRITUAL RENAISSANCE

BHARAT-KALYAN (COMPILED IN BENGALI) (7th ed)

HINDU DHARMA (BENGALI) (2nd ed)

HINDUISM
AT A GLANCE

BY
SWAMI NIRVEDANANDA

RAMAKRISHNA MISSION
CALCUTTA STUDENTS' HOME

Published by
Secretary,
Ramakrishna Mission Calcutta Students' Home
Belgharia, Kolkata-700056, West Bengal

First Edition, September 1944
Second Edition, January 1946
Third Edition, September 1957
Reprinted, September 1963
Fourth Edition (enlarged), January 1969
Reprinted, April 1979
Reprinted, May 1984
Eighth Edition, April 1993
Ninth Edition, August 1996
Reprinted, May 1998
Reprinted, April 2000
Reprinted, May 2004
Reprinted, May 2007
Reprinted, March 2010
Reprinted, June 2011
Reprinted, February 2013
Reprinted, June 2015

© *All rights reserved*

To be had of :
Advaita Ashrama
5 Dehi Entally Road, Kolkata-700014
&
Ramakrishna Math
Mylapore, Madras-600004

Printed by Rama Art Press
6/30 Dum Dum Road, Kolkata-700030

FOREWORD

THIS generation is loaded with a burden of fate as was hardly any other in the course of history. In previous periods of stress we had faith in certain general conceptions which gave us strength to stand the strain patiently. We have no such faith today. The increase of valid knowledge called science is having disturbing effects on religious traditions also. Only central truths as distinct from the dogmatic and institutional forms can appeal to the modern mind which is becoming increasingly rationalistic in temper and outlook. It is the author's conviction, which I share, that the essential principles of Hinduism have nothing to fear from any advance in scientific knowledge or historic criticism. In this small book which is directed not to the specialist, although based on specialized knowledge, but to the general educated reader, the author gives us a clear and precise account of the fundamental categories of Hindu thought. He has the gift of imparting information as if he were acquiring it. To my mind this book is an excellent introduction to the study of Hindu religion.

S. RADHAKRISHNAN

PREFACE TO THE FIRST EDITION

HINDUISM, resting on numerous and varied scriptural texts and covering a vast number of sectarian creeds, obviously requires an encyclopaedic treatment. *Hinduism at a Glance*, however, as the name suggests, is only a broad outline of the prominent features of this religion. It presents its essential contents in a nutshell, and aims at acquainting the busy reader with all that Hinduism stands for, and that as quickly as possible.

Though intended mainly for Hindu students, the book seeks to provide the interested public, including those living outside India, with necessary information on this ancient religion. The subject has been surveyed from a catholic standpoint, and the views of different current schools of Hindu thought have been treated with due regard. The first part dwells especially on the practical aspect of Hinduism and the second part on its ideology.

Certain Sanskrit words like *samsāra, mukti, bhuta* and *jiva* are closely associated with the Hindu Religion. A world of ideas hangs on these words. They serve almost as so many keys to Hindu thought. Through them one can enter into the spirit of Hinduism. But these words have no exact equivalents in English. This is why they have been used in the original. A clear grasp of their meaning will, no doubt, usher the reader into the domain of Hindu thought. Of course, these words have been explained in detail, often through distinct chapters, and in every case the nearest English rendering has been juxtaposed. Moreover, a glossary of all such words has been appended at the end of the book.

Sanskrit and other foreign words have been italicized, exception being made for names of persons, sects, communities, clans, castes, places and subjects of study. No diacritical marks could, however, be used for helping the correct pronunciation of Sanskrit words. Only where, except in the names of persons and places, 'a' has to be pronounced as in 'part', it has been italicized in words of Roman character and *vice versa*.

Sir S. Radhakrishnan has placed the author under a deep debt of gratitude by furnishing this book with an appropriate Foreword. Grateful acknowledgement is made to Swami Madhavananda, the Secretary of the Ramakrishna Mission, who has very kindly gone through the manuscripts.

Our labour will be justified if the book serves its purpose by fulfilling a real need throughout the English-knowing world.

September, 1944   NIRVEDANANDA

PREFACE TO THE SECOND EDITION

In this edition slight changes have been made in the body of the book. For helping correct pronunciation of Sanskrit words 'ā' has been used where 'a' has to be pronounced as in 'part', exception having been made in the cases of all names of persons and places. The letters 'jn' in a Sanskrit word have to be pronounced as hard 'gy' in English ; 'jnāna', for instance, has to be pronounced as 'gyāna', The letter 'e' in a Sanskrit word has always to be pronounced as 'e' in 'bed'.

January, 1946

N.

PUBLISHER'S NOTE

This "Reprint" comes out without any change. Meanwhile the book has been published in more than one major Indian language.

As in the fourth edition, 'ā' has been used in place of the long 'a' in all Sanskrit and allied words without any exception.

We have been compelled to raise the price of the book for obvious reasons.

May, 1984

S. D.

*   *   *

PUBLISHER'S NOTE TO THE NINETH EDITION

This "Edition" comes out without any change. Meanwhile the book has been published in more than one major Indian language.

As in the previous edition, 'ā' has been used in place of the long 'a' in all Sanskrit and allied words without any exception.

August 1996

Swami Amalananda

CONTENTS

LIST OF ABBREVIATIONS

Ait. Up.	— Aitareya Upanishad
Bh. Pr.	— Bhāgavata Purāna (Shrimad Bhāgavatam)
Br. S.	— Brahma Sutra
Bri. Up.	— Brihadāranyaka Upanishad
Ch. Chmta.	— Chaitanya Charitāmrita
Chh. Up.	— Chhāndogya Upanishad
Drg. Drs. Vk.	— Drig-Drishya Viveka
Ish. Up.	— Isha Upanishad
Ka. Up.	— Katha Upanishad
Kai. Up.	— Kaivalya Upanishad
Kau. Up.	— Kaushitaki Upanishad
Ke. Up.	— Kena Upanishad
Mātri. T.	— Mātrikābheda Tantra
Mats. Pr.	— Matsya Purāna
Mnv. Tr.	— Mahānirvāna Tantra
Mund. Up.	— Mundaka Upanishad
Rg. Vd.	— Rig-Veda
Shwet. Up.	— Shwetāshwatara Upanishad
Sw. Viv.'s Comp. Wks.	— Swāmi Vivekānanda's Complete Works
Tait. Up.	— Taittiriya Upanishad
Ved. Par.	— Vedānta Paribhāshā
Ved. Sār.	— Vedānta Sāra
Yg. S.	— Yoga Sutra

First Part

I

INTRODUCTION

HINDUISM is one of the major religions of the world. Its followers, numbering nearly four hundred millions, dwell in India[1] and they are known as the Hindus.

India has been the motherland of Hinduism for a long, long time. How long no one can say with precision. However, there is no doubt about the fact that Hinduism is several thousand years old, and that it is older than any other major religion of the world.

In very ancient days Hinduism was known as the Ārya *dharma* and its followers the Āryas. Their earliest home in India was in the Punjab. Nobody has yet been able to say finally where the Āryas of the Punjab had come from. Different scholars have made different guesses about the original home of the Aryas, such as the Arctic region, the great table-land of Central Asia, the Mediterranean coast, etc. Swāmi Vivekānanda was firm in his belief that the Āryas had not come from any place outside India.[2]

However, from the Punjab the Āryas gradually spread all over Northern India, which tract then

[1] Divided politically into India and Pakistan since 1947.
[2] See *Sw. Viv.'s Comp. Wks* (4th ed.) Vol. III, p. 293, Vol. IV, p. 333 and Vol. V, pp. 436–37.

came to be known as Āryāvarta. In course of time they crossed the Vindhya range and spread their religion in Southern India. An Ārya sage, Agastya by name, is said to have led this march of the Āryas to the South.

One may like to know how the Āryas came to be called the Hindus. The origin of the name Hindu is rather funny. The river Sindhu (Indus) marked the western frontier of the ancient Aryan settlement in the Punjab. On the other side of the river lived the ancient Iranians (Persians). It was by the name of this river that the Iranians called the Āryas. But they could not pronounce the word Sindhu correctly; they would pronounce it as Hindu. So Hindu came to be the name by which the Iranians called the Āryas. In course of time the Āryas themselves picked up this name from the Iranians.

The name Hindu also is very, very old. When the Hindus spread all over India, this entire country came to be known as Hindusthān.

Hindusthān has been the birthplace of many saints, many sages, many prophets. Through scores of centuries it has been prominently a land of religion. Its hills, mountains, rivers, lakes, seas and cities have been made holy by the touch of religion. These holy places strewn all over the country have made Hindusthān really a holy land. Through the ages myriads of pilgrims have been rushing to and fro from different corners of Hindusthān to visit these holy places. And religion has all along been the mainspring of the life of its people.

It was their religion that gave birth to the glorious culture of the Hindus. Even in the very ancient days the Hindus produced high class painting, sculpture, architecture, music and poetry. They wrote learned treatises on various subjects, such as Grammar, Philology, Logic, Philosophy, Politics, Astronomy (*Jyotisha*), Medicine and Surgery (*Āyurveda*). They put in valuable research work in Chemistry and have left behind sure proofs of their amazing skill in Engineering, Irrigation, Shipbuilding and in many other arts and crafts. And all these had their roots in religion; the ideas and ideals behind these were inspired mostly by Hindu saints.

In course of time, out of the great religion of the Hindus came two mighty offshoots, namely, Jainism and Buddhism. Hinduism together with its branch Buddhism spread even beyond the borders of Hindusthān. Countries like Ceylon, Burma, Siam, Cambodia, Cochin-China, Malaya, Java, Bali, Sumatra, China, Korea, Japan, Afghanistan and Turkestan came under the sway of one or both of these religions. Even in far off Mexico in North America scholars have detected traces of Hindu civilization. The people of these foreign lands hailed with delight the superior culture of the Hindus. The Hindus would never thrust their religion upon other people by force or stratagem. Peace, love, sympathy and service were their watchwords. Wherever they went they gave a lift to the people of the land from primitive life.

Surely, Hindusthān has been the mother of civilization in the East. And evidences[1] have already come up to prove that Hindu ideas travelled even to ancient Greece, the cradle of Western civilization.

In its march through scores of centuries Hinduism has been growing in bulk and variety. Within its fold there is now room for numerous sects, such as the Vaishnavas, the Shāktas, the Shaivas, the Sauras, the Gānapatyas, etc. Within each of these sects again there is room for numerous distinct groups. Moreover, the faiths of the Jainas, the Bauddhas, the Sikhs, the Ārya Samāj, the Brāhmo Samāj also are derived from Hinduism.

For some time past the hoary religion of the Hindus has been spreading its message in the far West. Many people in Europe and America are learning to esteem the Hindu view of life. Some of them are actually going so far as to adopt Hindu ideas and ideals.

Indeed the great religion of the Hindus is a mighty force for universal good. This is why this religion could have such a brilliant record of past achievements. And this is why the Hindus have reasons to believe that their religion is destined to have a more glorious future.

The following pages contain a brief *résumé* of the essential contents of this religion.

[1] *The Legacy of India.* (Ed. by G. T. Garratt), pp. 1–24.

II

DHARMA

WHAT THE HINDUS MEAN BY RELIGION

THE word 'religion' means a system of faith and worship. Belief in the tenets of a Church and performance of certain rituals prescribed by it are all that is required of a devout man by what is commonly known as religion in the West.

The Hindu word *dharma* appears to have a much deeper and wider meaning than the word 'religion'. Derived from the Sanskrit root *dhri* (to hold), *dharma* stands for that which holds up the existence of a thing. Everything in the universe has its *dharma*, because it must rely on something for its existence. And what is it on which the existence of a thing mainly depends? Well, it is the essential nature of a thing without which it can never exist. The essential nature of a thing, therefore, is called its *dharma*. Thus the power of burning is the *dharma* of fire; inertness is the *dharma* of all inanimate objects. Man also has an essential nature that upholds his existence as something distinct from the rest of creation. And this must be the *dharma* of man, that is, *mānava dharma*.

Now, what is the essential nature of man? The Hindus uphold that it is the power of becoming divine that marks out man from all other beings. This power, therefore, is *mānava dharma*.

But how is it possible for man to become divine? Because Divinity is already within him. Hinduism teaches that God is present everywhere.[1] He is also in our hearts. We are divine by nature. But Divinity lies deep in our being. We do not perceive It so long as our unclean mind stands in the way. Just as light cannot be seen through a smoky chimney, so God cannot be seen through an unclean mind, though all the while He is in us and everywhere about us. If we want light we have to cleanse the chimney; so if we want to bring out the Divinity in us, we have to cleanse our mind.

Lust, greed, anger, hatred, envy, pride, selfishness are so many impurities that obscure the Divinity within us. So long as these sway our mind, we make mistakes almost at every step of our life and very often behave exactly like brutes; our imperfection fills the cup of our misery and brings untold sufferings upon others.

Yes, it is due to these impurities that, at the start, we seem to stand on a level with the brutes. Yet we are not brutes. Why? Simply because we can work our way up to Divinity, which the brutes cannot. As men we are born with the power of removing all the impurities of our mind and becoming divine in all our bearings. This is precisely our

[1] Cf. *Ish. Up.* 1.

mānava dharma. Those who revel in these impurities have not yet emerged as men; they are only beasts in human form. While those who succeed in cleansing their minds thoroughly and bringing out the Divinity within them are real men, perfect men.

Of course, the path is long and the goal is far ahead. To bring out the Divinity in us completely is no easy job. The whole advance cannot be made by a single step. Yet it is a fact that a little progress on the path of *dharma* has its own reward. As our minds become purer, we grow wiser and get more strength and more joy. This inspires us to move forward and gradually increase our wisdom, strength and joy.

This process goes on from birth to birth till the mind becomes absolutely pure. It is then that man can see God, touch God, talk with God and can even become one with God. Then really man becomes perfect. For it is then that the Divinity that has all along been within him does manifest Itself completely.

Indeed the seer of God becomes truly divine, full of love, joy, wisdom and strength. He rises above nature and becomes absolutely free. Nothing can bind him or shake him. Nothing can disturb the peace of his mind. He has no want, no misery, no fear and no cause for strife or grief. His face always beams with divine joy and his conduct marks him out as a man of God. His selfless love

flows alike to all. His contact brings strength,
purity and solace to all who come near him. Verily
such a man has reached the goal of human life
and he alone may be said to be a truly religious
man or a perfect man.

The world has seen many such blessed seers of
God in different lands and different ages. They
are really the salt of the human race. Out of the
fulness of their hearts they preached what they
saw and felt. They taught all, who flocked to them,
the steps that had led them to realize God. These
teachings comprise the bulk of the religions of the
world.

The different seers, however, discovered different methods of cleansing the mind. Their teachings
are essentially alike. These vary only in minor
details. All true religions of the world lead us alike
to the same goal, namely, to perfection if, of course,
they are followed faithfully. Each of them is a
correct path to Divinity. The Hindus have been
taught to regard religion in this light.

Yes, according to the Hindu view there is
nothing wrong with the religions as they have been
preached by the prophets and seers of God. The
original teachings are priceless. They can give us
a sure and correct lead. These are the true religions
of the world.

But, unfortunately, what passes as religion in
the world often appears to contain more of husk

than of kernel. The spirit of the original teachings is buried under a heap of senseless dogmas. It comes to such a pass because very often religion is taken charge of by people who are not at all qualified for the task. Frequently people with impure minds pose as priests and preachers. They themselves cannot have any insight into things spiritual. They fail to grasp the import of the original teachings. And this is why, when they start explaining religion to others, they make a mess of the whole thing. In their hands religion degenerates into a mere creed, a bundle of crude dogmas and meaningless rituals. Their followers become wild and fanatic, and religion becomes a cause for communal fight. Instead of taking to religion for self-purification, the followers of different religions often engage themselves in breaking one another's heads. And this is called religion!

Such crude stuff naturally shocks the more sensible ones who, unfortunately, rush to give up religion altogether. But there are always some wise people in the world who cannot be duped by the unillumined priests. They see through the game; they find that the crudities of religion imported by ignorant priests and preachers lie just on the surface, beneath which there is priceless treasure.

Hinduism teaches us to distinguish this crude stuff from real religion. It warns us of the danger of being led by impostors and asks us to have religion

from the source, from the original teachings of the
seers and prophets. If these teachings require
explanation, that has to come from some other seer
of God. Not only this. Ḥinduism advises everyone
to find a seer to be his spiritual guide (*guru*).

We should not forget that religion is something
immensely practical. No amount of tall talk will
do. If we want to be real men we have to cleanse
our mind. This is precisely the task before us.
Simply to count oneself as a Hindu, or a Muslim, or
a Christian, is nothing. Merely to subscribe to the
views of a Church is not enough. Nor is it enough
to be only versed in one's religious lore. One has
to put into practice the teachings of the great seers
and prophets of one's own religion and regulate
one's entire life accordingly. This alone can lead
us towards the goal. We have to bring out the
Divinity within us and become real men, and for
this, we have to strive our best. Really, we attain
dharma, that is, our essential nature, only when
God in us becomes fully manifest. And for achieving this aim we should spare no pains.

Now, let us sum up what we have learnt from
this chapter. Everything in creation is essentially
divine.[1] It is given to man only to fully manifest
the Divinity within him and become divine in all
his bearings.[2] Then alone he attains perfection and
becomes a real man distinct from all other beings.

[1] Cf. *Chh. Up*. III. 14. 1.   [2] Cf. *Mund. Up*. III. 2. 9.

He enjoys unbounded freedom, bliss, power and wisdom. He can then speak like one in authority, and inspire others to go ahead. Religion teaches man how he can reach this blessed goal. Every religion, as it has been taught by its prophet or prophets, shows a correct path towards this goal. This is why religion is something immensely practical. We have to strive hard to carry out all that religion wants us to do. We have to form our attitude towards life and shape our conduct according to its teachings. If we go the other way and revel in our impurities, we sink to the brute level. These, in short, are some of the fundamental teachings of Hinduism, and from these we get a general idea of what the Hindus mean by religion.

III

THE HINDU SHĀSTRAS

THE teachings of the Hindu seers comprise the religion known as Hinduism or Hindu *dharma*. The holy texts that contain these teachings are known as the *Shāstras*.

Who is God? Where does He dwell? What does He look like? How are we related to Him? Why should we strive to realize Him? One may learn all these from the *Shāstras*. Moreover, the *Shāstras* teach us the methods of realizing God. How are we to bring out the Divinity within us? What are the obstacles in the way? How are we to get over them? How should we behave? What acts are we to perform? What acts are we to refrain from? The *Shāstras* teach us all these as well.

The Hindus have been treading the path of religion for scores of centuries. Throughout this period countless earnest souls have reached the goal of religion by realizing God. Many of these sages struck new paths leading to the same goal. Thus many methods of reaching perfection were discovered in this holy land by the Hindu sages. This is why the Hindu *Shāstras*, unlike the Scriptures of other religions, are many in number and variety. Moreover, the need of explaining religion to different classes of people gave rise to different classes of *Shāstras*.

VEDAS

Of these many and diverse Hindu *Shāstras*, the oldest are the Vedas. The rest derive their origin from the Vedas. The Vedas are based on direct revelation. This is why they are called *Shruti* and their authority is unquestioned. All other Hindu *Shāstras* owe their authority to the Vedas and are known as *Smriti*.

The Vedas are older than any other Scripture of the world. Derived from the Sanskrit root *vid* which means 'to know', the word *Veda* came to mean 'knowledge of God'. As the creation is infinite and eternal, so is the knowledge of God infinite and eternal. Hence, *Veda*, as knowledge of God, is inexhaustible and it exists eternally in the universe. Portions of this knowledge were discovered by hundreds of Hindu seers, and these we find recorded in what has come down to us as the Vedic texts. The Hindu seers who discovered these are known as the Vedic *rishis*. It is worth noticing that in the Vedas more prominence is given to the truths discovered than to the discoverers. As a matter of fact many of the *rishis* did not care even to leave their names behind.

The Vedas are four in number. They are known as *Rig-Veda*, *Sāma-Veda*, *Yajur-Veda* and *Atharva-*

Veda. Each of these consists of two sections, namely *Samhitā* and *Brāhmana*. The *Samhitā* section contains hymns or *mantras* and the *Brāhmana* section dwells on the meaning and use of these hymns.

The Hindus of yore would not worship gods and goddesses in images as we do now. Their worship consisted in reciting hymns (*mantras*) and offering oblations in sacred fire. This kind of worship is called *yajna* (sacrifice). The *Brāhmana* sections of the Vedas describe the various kinds of *yajna*. The *mantras* contained in the *Samhitā* sections have to be recited in course of the *yajnas*. From the *Brāhmana* sections one may learn when, how and which *mantras* have to be recited during the performance of any *yajna*.

UPANISHADS

Certain portions of the Vedas are known as the Upanishads. They are also called Vedānta, either because they occur towards the end of the Vedas, or because they contain the cream or essence of the Vedas.

The bulk of the Vedas deals with details related to *yajnas*. The *yajnas*, that is, the ancient modes of worship, are nothing but ceremonials to be performed for purifying one's mind so that it may become fit for receiving the knowledge of God. Hence this portion of the Vedas concerned mainly with ceremonials (*karma*) is known as the *Karma-*

kānda. On the other hand, the portions of the Vedas known as the Upanishads dwell primarily on the knowledge of God. This is why they constitute what is known as the *Jnāna-kānda* of the Vedas.

Where and how does God exist? How are man and the universe related to Him? How and why should one try to realize God? What does exactly happen when one realizes Him? All these may be learnt from the Upanishads (or Vedānta).

The Upanishads are many in number. Each of the four Vedas contains several Upanishads. Of these, the following may be remembered: *Isha*, *Kena*, *Katha*, *Prashna*, *Mundaka*, *Māndukya*, *Aitareya*, *Taittiriya*, *Chhāndogya*, *Brihadāranyaka* and *Shwetā-shwatara*.

SMRITIS

Some sages like Manu and Yājnavalkya compiled codes or manuals of Hindu life. These are known particularly as *Smritis*, though the term *Smriti* in a broader sense covers all Hindu *Shāstras* except the Vedas. From these *Smritis* by Manu, Yājnavalkya and other sages a Hindu learns how he has to spend his entire life. They instruct him as to how he should behave at different periods of his life (*āshrama*), and also what special duties are enjoined on him due to his birth in a particular social group (*varna*). These also describe all ceremonies connected with the domestic life of a Hindu.

Moreover, these lay down domestic and social laws for the Hindus.

These *Smritis*, in short, prescribe certain acts and prohibit some others for a Hindu according to his birth and stage of life. Their sole object is to purify the mind gradually so that one may advance step by step towards perfection. They are no doubt based on the teachings of the Vedas. Yet it is to be noted that their injunctions (*vidhi*) and prohibitions (*nishedha*) are related to the particular social surroundings. As these surroundings of the Hindu society changed from time to time, new *Smritis* had to be compiled by the sages of different ages and different parts of Hindusthan. Thus Raghunandana's *Smriti* is of a much later age than Manu's and it is applicable particularly to the Hindu society of Bengal. As our present-day society has changed considerably since the days of the last Smriti-maker, time is perhaps ripe for a fresh *Smriti* for the Hindus of our days.

DARSHANAS

The knowledge of God found in the Vedas gave rise to six different schools of thought. The sages, Jaimini, Vyāsa, Kapila, Patanjali, Gotama and Kanāda introduced these different schools. Each of them wrote what is known as a Darshana; and the six together are known as *Shad-Darshana. Purva Mimānsā, Uttara Mimānsā (Vedānta), Sāmkhya, Yoga,*

Nyāya and *Vaisheshika* are the six Darshanas named in order of their authors mentioned above. Each of these is written in a peculiar style, namely, in aphorisms (*sutras*). The *sutras* of Sanskrit grammar remind one of the style of the Darshanas. These terse *sutras* of the Darshanas require explanation and these naturally gave rise, in the course of time, to a vast number of notes and commentaries on each of the Darshanas.

Of these Darshanas, the *Purva Mimānsā* deals with the *Karma-kānda* of the Vedas and the *Uttara Mimānsā* with the *Jnāna-kānda*. The latter is derived directly from the Upanishads. This Darshana composed by the great sage Vyāsa is also known as *Vedānta Darsana* or *Brahma Sutras*. This may be said to be one of the cornerstones of the Hindu religion. Great saints like Sri Shankarāchārya and Sri Rāmānujāchārya in later days wrote brilliant commentaries on this *Vedānta Darshana*.

PURĀNAS

The Darshanas are no doubt very stiff. They are meant only for the learned few. For the common folk another class of *Shāstras* was brought out by the Hindu sages. These *Shāstras* are called the Purānas. Through these, religion is taught in a very easy and interesting way. The teachings are driven home through inspiring stories and parables. Moreover, glimpses of the ancient history of Hindusthān may be had through the Purānas. We have eighteen Purānas in all. Of these, the names of the following may be remembered: *Vishnu Purāna, Padma Purāna, Vāyu Purāna, Skanda Purāna, Agni Purāna, Mārkandeya Purāna* and *Bhāgavata.* A portion of the *Mārkandeya Purāna* is well-known to all Hindus as *Devi-Māhātmyam* or *Chandi.* Worship of God as the Divine Mother is its theme. It is read widely by the Hindus on sacred days.

RĀMĀYANA AND MAHĀBHĀRATA

Like the Purānas the *Rāmāyana* and the *Mahābhārata* are two very popular and useful *Shāstras of* the Hindus. These are two epics (Mahākāvya) produced by the sages Vālmiki and Vyāsa, respectively. They are classed as Itihāsas (histories) and they give us interesting stories through which all the essential teachings of Hinduism are stamped on one's mind. These have been translated in many Indian languages. It is through these translations that the bulk of the Hindus get acquainted with their religion.

GITĀ

A portion of the *Mahābhārata* is known as the *Gitā.* The *Mahābhārata* describes the battle of Kurukshetra. The Kauravas and their cousins, the Pāndavas, were the contending parties. Of the five Pāndava princes, Arjuna was the third and the greatest hero. *Bhagavān* Sri Krishna chose to be his charioteer. Just on the eve of the great battle *Bhagavān* Sri Krishna explained the essentials of Hindu religion to Arjuna. This section of the *Mahābhārata* containing the teachings of *Bhagavān* Sri Krishna is known as *Shrimad-Bhagavad-Gitā*. Just as the Upanishads contain the cream of the Vedas, so does the *Gitā* contain the cream of the Upanishads. Of all Hindu *Shāstras*, the *Gitā* has come to be by far the most popular one.

PRASTHĀNATRAYA

The Upanishads, the *Vedānta Darshana* and the *Gitā* are grouped together and called the *Prasthānatraya*. These are looked upon as the basic Scriptures of the Hindu religion. They are highly authoritative. The founders of the important sects of Hinduism had to base their teachings on the *Prasthānatraya*. Only they interpreted it in different ways and came to different conclusions, such as *Advaita-vāda* (monism), *Vishistādvaita-vāda* (qualified monism) and *Dvaita-vāda* (dualism).

TANTRAS

There is yet another group of *Shāstras* known as the Tantras. These dwell on the *Shakti* (energy) aspect of God and prescribe numerous courses of ritualistic worship[1] of the Divine Mother in various

---

[1] See *infra* Chap. XII.

forms. The texts are usually in the form of dialogues between *Shiva* and *Pārvati*. In some of these *Shiva*, as the teacher, answers the questions put by *Pārvati*; in others the goddess is the teacher answering *Shiva's* questions. The former texts are known as Āgama and the latter as Nigama. There are numerous Tantras, of which sixty-four are said to be prominent. The following may be remembered: *Mahānirvāna*, *Kulārnava*, *Kulasāra*, *Prapanchasāra*, *Tantrarāja*, *Rudra Yāmala*, *Brahma Yāmala*, *Vishnu Yāmala* and *Todala Tantras*.

PANCHARĀTRA SAMHITĀS AND SHAIVA ĀGAMAS

Allied to the Tantras are the Pancharātra Samhitās of the Vaishnavas and the Shaiva Āgamas.[1] Like the Tantras, these also claim to present easier cults and doctrines more suited to this age (*Kali Yuga*) than the Vedas. Unlike the other *Shāstras* mentioned above, these do not derive their authority from the Vedas, to which, however, they are not openly hostile. Another feature of this group of sacred texts is that they are open to all castes and both the sexes after they are initiated (*dikshita*).

Of the Pancharātra Samhitās, though two hundred and fifteen separate texts are mentioned, the names of the following may very well be

---

[1] Vide *A History of Indian Literature* by Winternitz, Vol. I. p. 587.

remembered: *Ishwara, Paushkara, Parama, Sāttwata, Brihad-Brahma* and *Jnānāmritasāra Samhitās*.[1]

There is a traditional list of twenty-eight Shaiva Āgamas, each with a number of Upāgamas. Of these, however, only fragmentary texts of twenty are extant.

---

[1] The first of these was referred to by Yāmunāchārya, the next three by Rāmānujāchārya; the last has been published under the title *Nārada Pancharātra*.

IV

SAMSĀRA

REBIRTH AND KARMAVĀDA

THE word *samsāra* in the Hindu lexicon is very significant. We are all familiar with this word, yet we hardly know what it exactly means. We use the word loosely to mean either the world or worldly life. It is derived from the Sanskrit root *sri* which means passing and its prefix *sam* means intensely. Now, our *Shāstras* teach us that we have to pass repeatedly through this world and other finer and higher worlds.[1] This repeated passing of souls (*samsriti*) is what is really meant by the word *samsāra*.

The whole of Hinduism takes its stand on this idea of *samsāra*. And it gives a clue to the entire Hindu view of life. Why do we offer oblations to our departed relatives? Because we believe that they are still living either in any of the fine worlds or on this earth in some other bodies. Why does a Hindu woman take the vow of widowhood after the demise of her husband? Because she hopes to meet her husband after her death only if she can remain faithful to him. The Hindus perform meritorious deeds (*punya*), for these, they believe,

[1] Cf. *Gita* VIII. 16.

will bring them intense enjoyment after death. They try to shun heinous deeds (*pāpa*) lest they should have intense sufferings after death. These and many other beliefs and rites are derived from the Hindu idea of rebirth. And this idea is no fiction. It rests on facts realized by the Hindu seers.

So this idea of rebirth is a very important thing in the Hindu view of life. We should, therefore, try to have a very clear grasp of this, before we proceed any further in our study of Hinduism.

We shall not cease to exist after death. Before this birth all of us have passed through innumerable lives. In the *Gitā Bhagavān* Sri Krishna says to Arjuna, "O Arjuna, both you and I have had many births before this, (only) I know them all, while you do not."[1] He again says, "Birth is inevitably followed by death and death by rebirth."[2] Indeed, one is born in this world again and again till the Divinity within is completely manifested. Each time one is born with a new body which lasts for a while and then wears off and drops dead. But that which resides within the body remains as fresh as ever. It simply moves out of the decayed and useless body and remains for a time in finer worlds. After that it comes to this world and gets a fresh body. The finer worlds are meant for intense enjoyment or suffering. That is why they are called *bhogabhumi* (land of experience). It is

[1] *Ibid*. IV. 5.   [2] *Ibid*. II. 27.

this world where everyone has to come to work out his perfection. This world, therefore, is called *karmabhumi* (land of action). So long as one does not attain perfection one is bound to go through repeated births. Till then one is in a state of bondage (*baddha*). The necessity of passing over and over through the worlds (*samsāra*) is itself the bondage.

At each birth we get a fresh body. This body is made of matter and is called *sthula sharira* (gross body). It is built out of the materials taken as food and is, therefore, also called *annamaya kosha* (covering made of food). This gross body is our outermost cover. One lives in this body just as one lives in a house. When the house collapses, one gets out of it and builds another house to live in. So also when this gross body becomes useless, one leaves it and builds a fresh body. In the *Gita* this body has been compared to a piece of cloth. When the cloth wears out, one rejects it and gets a fresh one for use; so also when the body becomes useless, one passes out of it and reappears in a fresh body.[1] This giving up of a decayed and useless body is what we call death, and reappearance in a fresh body is called rebirth. Thus by death and rebirth we simply change worn-out bodies for fresh ones. Everyone of us has done this times without number. Those who know this truth have nothing to fear or grieve for.

[1] Cf. *ibid.* II. 22.

Inside this gross body we have yet another finer and stronger body in which we live. This is called *sukshma sharira*, the fine body. Neither disease, nor old age, nor death can touch this fine body. Nothing in nature can destroy it. Through our countless births in the past our fine bodies have been our constant companions.

The fine body consists of seventeen parts, namely, *buddhi* (intellect), *manas* (mind), five *prānas*[1] (vital energy) and the finer counterparts of the ten sense-organs.[2] It is this fine body that builds up the gross one and keeps it going. Through it we feel, think and desire. Indeed, this fine body is the active part of our being.

Yet the fine body is not active by itself. It is as inert as the gross body, though the latter is animated and made to work by it. It is itself animated and made to work by something else. This something is the true Self of man. This is his *Ātman* (Soul).

The *Ātman* is the source of all life, activity and consciousness (*chaitanya*).[3] Warmed up into life by Its touch, the fine body animates the gross one just as the moon illuminated by the sun lights up this earth.

---

[1] See *infra* Chap. XVI, foot-note.
[2] Ten sense-organs: *Jnānendriya* (organs of perception)—eyes, ears, nose, tongue, and skin.
    Karmendriya (organs of action)—hands, feet, tongue, organ of elimination and organ of reproduction.
[3] Cf. *Drg. Drs. Vk.* XVI.

Thus animated by the *Ātman* the fine body works the grosser one as long as it can and then leaves it and builds up a fresh body. In this way we proceed from birth to birth.

KARMAVĀDA

But why has one to be born again and again? The Hindu *Shāstras* are very clear on this point. The Divinity in man reveals Itself only when the mind becomes spotlessly clean. But this takes a long, long time. One gross body cannot last long. Our lifetime is too short for this task. That is why we have to go through innumerable births before this task is done.

There are so many things in this world that please our senses and so many that repel them. Hence we desire to have certain things and to avoid certain others. Our minds are always full of such desires. To fulfil these desires we exert our-selves. Our life consists of such exertions. Yet we can never exhaust our desires. They go on multi-plying. When we fulfil one desire, the hunger of our senses for enjoyment becomes keener; and this gives rise to a crop of fresh desires. Thus we go on doing things for fulfilling our never-ending desires.

Now, whatever we do in this way is sure to bring either pleasure or pain as its effect. Each deed (*karma*) is destined to bear a fruit (*karma-phala*), sooner or later. A good or meritorious deed (*shubha karma*) brings pleasure as its effect and an evil deed (*ashubha karma*) brings pain. Men usually have both good and bad desires. These lead them to perform both meritorious and evil deeds and thus to pile up both pleasure and pain as their consequence (*karma-phala*).

During each lifetime we exhaust only a portion of our past *karma-phala*. This portion is called *prārabdha*. The remainder that has to be tasted in future lives is called *samchita*. The fruits of our present deeds will lie stored up as *kriyamāna*. Hence, for reaping the fruits of our own actions, we have to go from birth to birth.

A child is born blind. His blindness is surely due to some physical cause. But his mental agony owing to his blindness, according to the Hindu *Shāstras*, must be ascribed to some particular misdeed in any of his previous lives. When, in spite of our best efforts, we fail in any of our endeavours, we usually curse our fate (*adrishta*). Or when without any effort we meet with an unexpected success, we hail our luck (*adrishta*) with delight. This *adrishta* (unseen), however, is nothing but the fruit of our own past actions, our own *karma-phala*. We need neither curse it nor hail it. This comes as a matter of course, as a sure result of our past deeds. We cannot avoid the pleasure and pain caused by our own acts (*karma*) during past lives. We have produced them. We have made the bed and we must lie on it. We have no right to curse anything or anybody for our griefs and ailments.

But we can do one thing. We can make our future lives happy. That depends on our present efforts. We are the builders of our own future. If we avoid the evil deeds prohibited by the *Shāstras* and go on performing good ones enjoined by them, then we shall surely have a happy future.

This, in short, is what Hinduism teaches us about *karma* (*Karmavāda*). Our desires (*kāma*) produce *karma*, *karma* produces its fruits as pain or pleasure, and to reap the fruits of our *karma* we have to go from birth to birth. In this way our desires whirl us through the almost interminable round of births and deaths that we call *samsāra*.

V

MUKTI

LIBERATION

WE have seen how our desires drag us through repeated births and deaths. We have no option in the matter. As long as we shall be seeking anything of this world or the next we shall be forced to go through this round of births and deaths. This journey called *samsāra* seems to be an endless affair. And it is very painful, too.

The world offers us many pleasant things no doubt. But they never give us satiety. No attainment is enough for us. Whatever be our position, we want more power, more knowledge, more happiness. This desire goes on increasing and gives us no rest. The thought of achieving something haunts us always and makes us feel uneasy. Moreover, along with sense-enjoyment we have to carry a very heavy burden of sorrow. Failure and disappointment, loss and separation, disease and death have to be endured by all. All these make our life through repeated births very painful.

Is there no escape from this? Is there no way out of this continued life of misery and frustration? The Hindu *Shāstras* answer in the affirmative.

Yes, there is a way out. We can do away with all miseries by realizing God. For then alone we

shall find what we have been seeking all along,
namely, eternal bliss and infinite knowledge. And
we shall have no longer to go through birth and
death. We shall be freed, once for all, from *samsāra*.

This state of liberation from *samsāra* is called
mukti. The liberated man (*mukta purusha*) realizes
the essence of his being as none other than God,
and, therefore, becomes divine in all his bearings.
Eternal peace reigns in his heart. He has no want,
no misery, no fear. Love and compassion for all
move him to help them out of *samsāra.*

The Hindu *Shāstras* hold that liberation (*mukti*)
is the goal to be attained by every individual.
Indeed, everyone is terribly earnest to reach this
goal. Only he may not be aware of this fact.

Whenever we exert to extend our power,
knowledge and happiness, whenever we try to
escape from death, we really want to bring out
the Divinity within us. And we are doing this all
the time. We refuse to remain within the bounds
of Nature. Nature gives us only interrupted glimpses
of joy, knowledge, power and life. But in our Soul
we have all these in an unbounded measure. For
our Soul is essentially one with God. And this is
why the little morsels of joy, knowledge, power and
life we have to wrest from Nature (*Prakriti*) by
our hard struggles never satisfy us.[1] And our search
for these things ends only when we come to fully

[1] Cf. *Chh. Up.* VII. 23.

realize and manifest the divinity of our Soul. Reaching the infinite ocean of Existence, Knowledge and Bliss (*Satchidānanda-sāgara*), we have no longer to hanker after the little drops doled out by Nature.

Thus, consciously or unconsciously, every creature on earth is led forward by the instinctive urge for realizing the Eternal and Infinite One within it. In other words, everyone is hurrying to attain *mukti* (liberation) from this *samsāra*.

Now, aimless wandering through *samsāra* is no good. It prolongs our state of bondage. If all our aspirations come to be fulfilled only by attaining liberation, we ought to know that from the very beginning. It saves us a lot of trouble. This is why the Hindus are made aware of *mukti* (liberation) as the goal to be reached and they are exhorted to bend their steps towards it from the very start.

To attain this, however, is no easy job. The path is long and hard. We have to realize God, for then alone shall we be completely liberated. True, God is always within us and all about us. But so long as our minds are unclean, we cannot realize Him. So we have to cleanse our minds and that is about all we have to do till we reach the goal. This is our practical religion (*dharma*), our *sādhanā* (spiritual endeavour).

This cleaning of the mind is a long-drawn process. The time required for this cannot be measured by months and years. It may take numerous births before one reaches the goal.[1]

The Hindu *Shāstras* assure us, however, of one thing. The progress made in one life is not lost. The next birth begins with this as an asset. Moreover, these *Shāstras* prescribe a graded course of mental purification. All minds are not in the same state of purification because their present state is determined by their efforts in previous births. This is why we differ from one another so much in our capacity, taste and temperament. Some minds are crude, some are refined. In Hinduism each finds a starting-point suited to its stage of purification.

Now, let us see what purification of the mind exactly means. Our minds seem to be glued to the world. We have to focus them entirely on God and on nothing else. One's mind has to be drawn away from sense-objects and fixed on God. Then alone one is sure to realize God and become free for ever.

But our senses are attracted by the charming things of this world and the higher ones. Our minds run after the senses and we forget everything about God and our aim in life.[2] It is no easy task for us to draw our minds away from their mad pursuit of attractive things.

Yet it has to be done, no matter how long we

[1] Cf. *Gitā* VI. 45.   [2] Cf. *ibid* II. 67.

may have to strive. Attachment to all sense-objects
has to be given up.[1] This can be achieved by
sincere and persevering efforts. As this attachment
decreases our minds get closer and closer to God.
They are like so many iron filings covered up with
the mud of attachment, as it were. As they are
cleansed, God attracts them like a mighty magnet.

Now, attachment to all sense-objects cannot be
given up in a day. Even the idea of such a thing
is shocking to many. Crude minds, like little
children, want to enjoy the world. They need not
go in for all-out detachment. Hinduism prescribes
for them a preliminary course. This is known as
the *Pravritti Mārga* (the Path of Desire). It allows
individuals to desire the good things of this world
and the higher ones and tells them how they may
fulfil such desires. Those who follow this path
sincerely can minimize their misery and obtain a
good deal of enjoyment here and hereafter. Not
only this, they get their minds gradually purified
to a certain extent by this process. For the *Pravritti
Mārga* is essentially an elementary course of mental
discipline. The *Karma-kānda* (the section dealing
with rituals) of the Vedas shows this path and the
Purva Mimānsā explains the details.

Then there are others who appear to be fed up
with this world. They do not hanker even after
the intense enjoyment of the sense-objects of the

[1] Cf. *ibid.* VI. 35.

higher worlds. Their experience in this life and the previous ones must have helped them to see through the hollowness of sense-enjoyment. These people are fit for taking up the final course, and that is the *Nivritti Mārga* (the Path of Renunciation). Renouncing all desires, they have to concentrate their minds absolutely on God. Various methods for doing this are prescribed. One may take up any of these and advance straight to the goal. The *Jnāna-kānda* (the section dealing with knowledge) of the Vedas consisting of the Upanishads is the earliest revealer of this path.

Thus Hinduism teaches us to ascend to perfection by two stages. The Path of Desire (*Pravritti Mārga*) followed in due time by the Path of Renunciation (*Nivritti Mārga*) covers the whole course. The course ends only when the last trace of attachment to worldly things drops off and the Divinity in us becomes fully manifest. For then alone we get out of *samsāra* and attain *mukti*.

VI

PRAVRITTI MĀRGA

THE PATH OF DESIRE

THE world is so charming. It is full of things that make for our enjoyment. Pleasing sights, sounds, smells, tastes and touches attract us. We want to seize them and enjoy them. Our desire for such enjoyment goes on increasing.

Then again, there are infinitely more charming things in the finer worlds. Just think of a learned, honest and optimistic young man with a strong and sound body ruling over the whole world and having all its riches and objects of enjoyment at his disposal. Can you imagine how happy he is? Yet his happiness is nothing compared with what one may get in the finer worlds. You have to multiply his happiness one million times to measure the happiness of a soul in the *Pitriloka*. This again multiplied one million times will give a measure of the happiness in the *Devaloka*. The same process over again will show what happiness one enjoys in the *Brahmaloka*. This is how our *Shāstras* have put it.[1]

Thus informed by the *Shāstras*, we become eager to enjoy the intensely pleasing things of the

[1] Cf. *Tait. Up.* II. 8. 1–4.

finer worlds as well. We desire, therefore, to get the best things of this world as also of the finer worlds.

Our *Shāstras* show us the way of fulfilling such desires. This is the Path of Desire (*Pravritti Mārga*). They teach us that we have to scan our desires. Each and everyone of them is not good. Some lead us to evil deeds which bring misery as their sure effect. We have to drop those desires if we want to be happy. Thus lying, stealing, cheating, inflicting injury upon others are all evil deeds. They react upon us by bringing in miseries. We must avoid these. Any desire that prompts us to perform such evil deeds has to be given up. Our *Shāstras* prohibit all acts that bring us misery. Those who want happiness here and hereafter should never go against the prohibitions (*nishedha*) of the *Shāstras*.

Then again, our *Shāstras* enjoin us to do certain meritorious deeds. For these are sure to bring happiness. So long as we are on the Path of Desire (*Pravritti Mārga*), we should spare no pains to carry out these injunctions (*vidhi*) of the *Shāstras*.

Now, what is the nature of a meritorious deed? In a word, any act that helps us to become unselfish is a meritorious one. Such acts alone can bring one happiness. One has to pay for one's future happiness out of one's present selfish interests. Each of these acts is a sacrifice, is what is called a *yajna*.

PANCHA-YAJNA

Our *Shāstras* prescribe five acts of sacrifice (*yajnas*) for all. These are *Deva-yajna*, *Pitri-yajna*, *Rishi-yajna*, *Nri-yajna* and *Bhuta-yajna*. We have to please the dwellers of the *Devaloka* and *Pitriloka*, the seers and makers of *Shāstras*, mankind and all other creatures on earth by our acts of sacrifice. We have to give all others something out of what we have. This is the price of our happiness.

Prayer and worship please the deities (*devas*). These deities are also creatures like ourselves. Only they are more well-placed. Once they were men. As a reward for their good deeds on earth they have been born as gods in the *Devaloka*. They have considerably more power than we have. They control the elemental forces of nature like light, heat, electricity, rain, wind, etc. When pleased by our offerings, they make these forces favourable to us and bless us with what we desire most.

Among the dwellers of the *Pitriloka* there may be many of our forefathers. They love us. If we remember them and offer them oblations (*tarpana*) they become pleased (*tripta*). They also wield much more power than we do. That is why when they are pleased they can bless us with the things of our desire.

The seers (*rishis*) do not want any material offering from us. They are pleased if we study the Scriptures regularly. *Nitya-karma*, like *Sandhyā-Van-*

danā, also may go under this head. For these we have to set apart a portion of our time. This is why this study (*swādhyāya*) is also an act of sacrifice. When pleased, the seers, like *devas*, see to our well-being.

Nri-yajna is the fourth in order. We have to serve our ailing brothers. We should try to remove the distress of our fellow-beings. One who does this really serves God. For God is here in so many forms. Pleased by such service, God grants one's wishes.

The same thing may be said of *Bhuta-yajna*, which comes next. We should spare a portion of our food for the beasts, birds, insects, etc. This act of sacrifice also earns for us happiness.

The first two *yajnas* consist of sacrificial rites and the last two, of acts of charity; and these four together are known as *ishtāpurta*.[1]

VARNĀSHRAMA DHARMA

Besides the five *yajnas*, everyone has certain duties to perform according to his stage of life and station in society. Hindu life is divided into four stages (*āshramas*), namely, *Brahmacharya, Gārhasthya, Vānaprastha* and *Sannyāsa*. Student life, householder's life, retired life and life of renunciation—these are the four stages coming one after the other. For each of these stages (*āshramas*) certain specific

---

[1] *Ishta*—Sacrificial rites.
Purta—Acts of charity, like the excavation of public wells.

duties are enjoined. Then there are four social
groups, each having a separate code of duties.
The Brāhmanas (spiritual teachers and law-
makers), the Kshatriyas (warriors), the Vaishyas
(traders) and the Shudras (labourers) are the four
social groups (*varnas*). Those who are to study and
explain the *Shāstras* are the Brāhmanas; they are
enjoined to lead strictly pure and simple lives. The
Kshatriyas are the kings and warriors. They are
not to abuse their power. Their arms are meant
for the protection of the weak and punishment of
the wicked. The Vaishyas or merchants are not to
stoop to greed or dishonesty. They are to spend
according to their might for charities. The Shudras
or labourers are taught to be upright and active.

Now, for getting the pleasing things of this
world and of the next, one has to carry out all the
duties related to one's *varna* and *āshrama*. The
duties of each according to his social standing and
stage of life comprise his own religion (*swadharma*).

Over and above the five yajnas and the
varnāshrama duties, we have to worship God and
pray to Him for the things we desire. God is
really the Dispenser of the fruits of our actions.
He fulfils our desires if we pray to Him earnestly
after having done all our duties faithfully. We
have to exert ourselves as much as we can for
gaining the desired object. For it is then and then
only that our sincere prayers to God are answered.

Thus, besides the moral discipline through the practice of truth, non-stealing, non-injury, etc., the five *yajnas*, the *varnāshrama* duties and worship of God are enjoined on all who want to tread the Path of Desire (*Pravritti Mārga*). The *yajnas* teach us sacrifice and service. They teach us to love and serve fellow-beings and all beings above and below us. God is all love and He is in all beings. So, by performing these *yajnas*, we gradually come out of the dark cave of selfishness and get nearer to God, the source of all love and light. The *yajnas*, therefore, not only bring us happiness but also lead us from darkness towards light by purifying our minds. The *varnāshrama* duties also go to remove many of our impurities. These help us gradually to shake off our lethargy (*tamas*) and to control our passions (*rajas*), Lastly, nothing purifies our minds more than the thought of God. Whenever we think of Him our minds become purer.

VII

PRAVRITTI MĀRGA (*continued*)

AS IT IS

We have seen how the Hindus of old would strive to secure happiness in this life and the next. The main idea was to chasten one's mind through gradual self-control, sacrifice, service and devotion to God. And the ancient Hindus would go through such discipline for the sake of earning enjoyment here and hereafter.

That some amount of moral and spiritual discipline contributes to our pleasures here and hereafter is an eternal truth discovered by the ancient *rishis*. And on this is based the *Pravritti Mārga* or the Path of Desire. This truth is as effective in our days as in the days of old. We need have no doubt regarding this.

Yet we should notice one thing. Through the ages vast changes have come over the details of Hinduism. Though the central truth of the Path of Desire persists, the forms of discipline have undergone radical changes.

Take, for instance, the *Deva-yajna*. Formerly they used to offer oblations of butter, curd, etc. intended for various deities to fire. And while doing this they would recite hymns of the deities and utter appropriate *mantras* (sacred formulae).

The hymns and *mantras* as well as the entire procedure would be taken from the Vedas.

In our days we worship the deities usually with light, incense, flowers, fruits, sweets and other such things, accompanied by *mantras* and hymns of a different kind. Moreover, we have before us images or symbols[1] of the deities and before these we make our offerings. Our Vedic forefathers had no such things. The *mantras* to be recited as well as the entire procedure are supplied by later (mostly Tāntric) *Shāstras*.[2] *Yajna*, as oblations in fire, persists often only as a part of ceremonial worship. On rare occasions, however, pure Vedic *yajnas*, like the *Putreshti-yāga*, are even now performed by some people with specific ends in view.[3]

Then again, most of the Vedic deities like *Indra*, *Vāyu*, *Varuna*, *Mitra* and *Ashwinikumāras* have receded to the background. Some of them still abide only in connection with ceremonial worship. Long ago the Vedic deities were thrown into the shade by *Surya*, *Ganapati*, *Vishnu*, *Shiva* and the Divine Mother (*Shakti*). God came to be worshipped in these forms. This gave rise to five sects, namely, Saura, Gānapatya, Vaishnava, Shaiva and Shākta. Each sect worshipped God in

---

[1] Such as the *Shālagrāma-shilā* representing *Vishnu* or *Shivalinga* representing *Shiva*. See *infra* Chap. XI.

[2] See *infra* Chap. XII.

[3] The pure form of Vedic worship has been revived by the Arya Samāj founded by Swāmi Dayānanda.

one of these forms. In our days the last three sects predominate.

From the earliest days the Hindus have had a vision of unity. We know that God is one and that He may be worshipped in any of His forms or even without any form. God sanctions the fruits of our action. If we stick to the righteous path and pray to God, we are sure to get what we seek from Him. We may or may not go in for appeasing the different deities. Our prayers may be addressed straight to God. Nothing else in the form of *Deva-yajna* remains to be done.[1] So worship of God in one or more forms or without any form has come to replace the ancient *Deva-yajna*.

Now let us turn to the *varnāshrama* duties. Our social structure has changed almost beyond recognition. Formerly there were four *varnas*— Brāhmana, Kshatriya, Vaishya and Shudra.[2] The ancient Hindu society was divided into these four groups according to their different qualifications and vocations. Each group had its prescribed duties. In place of the four *varnas* we have developed hundreds of castes and sub-castes, though true Brāhmanas and true Kshatriyas are rarely to be found. Birth alone determines our caste. Qualification and vocation have almost nothing to do with

[1] Of course, *nitya-karma* like *Sandhyā-Vandanā*, including repetition of the *Gāyatri*, is still in vogue.
[2] Cf. *Gitā* IV. 13.

our castes. Prohibition of intermarriage, interdining, etc. keeps the castes apart. Untouchability also plays no mean part in this affair. This aspect of our Hindu society at the moment is very sad. It has bred hatred. It is dragging us down from the original Hindu ideal of universal love. The *varnāshrama* duties were meant for self-purification. Our caste ideas do the reverse. If we should retain our castes, we must at least see that hatred of our fellow-men is banished altogether. Neither the individuals nor the society will be benefited by the prejudices that have grown around the caste system.

The four *āshramas*, namely, *Brahmacharya*, *Gārhasthya*, *Vānaprastha* and *Sannyāsa*, were four successive stages of an individual's life. These stages, each with its specific duties, formed a graded course of spiritual growth. Such a system shows that the life of an ancient Hindu was a continued striving for spiritual progress. Everything else in life was tuned to this supreme objective.

This was an ideal state of things. It made the best of human life. Such training tended to eliminate all that was antisocial. Thus both the individual and the society gained considerably by this process.

In the present-day Hindu society an individual usually passes through only one *āshrama*, namely *Gārhasthya*. Even there the idea of the *Gārhasthya āshrama* with its specific duties is absent. Student life no longer comes under the *Brahmacharya āshrama*. The life of a *Sannyāsi* still exists, though only as an exception to the general custom.

Now this slip from the *varnāshrama* system measures the depth of our fall from the Hindu ideals of old. Our outlook has been shifted from the spiritual to the secular. Duty-consciousness is being replaced very fast by right-consciousness. We do not feel the necessity of qualifying ourselves spiritually for gaining the things of our desire. We simply demand them and fight for them. Survival of the fittest is our slogan. But this is only a law of the jungle. It does not work where spiritual evolution is desired.

Thus the original scheme of Hindu life has come to be almost upset by the intrusion of un-spiritual motives. Spiritual discipline, which is the *sine qua non* of Hindu life, is tending to become conspicuous by its absence.

AS IT SHOULD BE

This is a very sad state of spiritual degradation. We must have faith in our *Shāstras* and rebuild our society on the ancient ideas and ideals. All that we have to do is to readjust the details to suit our changed surroundings.

It may not be possible now to regroup our society under the four *varnas*. Yet it is possible to see that those who take up the vocations corresponding to any of the four groups should devoutly perform the duties prescribed for the same. Those, for instance, who choose the vocation of a priest or religious preacher, must try earnestly to acquire the qualifications of a Brāhmana as described in the *Shāstras*. Those who take up arms as their vocation have to follow the Kshatriya code as laid down in our Scriptures. This also has to be done by those whose vocations correspond to those of the Vaishyas and the Shudras. Of course, details may be modified, if necessary, to suit the changed conditions.

So far as the four *āshramas* are concerned, they should be revived as soon as possible. This is a treasure we have lost. Our Hindu society is bound to become hollow and to crumble down if we delay any longer to restore at least the first three *āshramas*. The last may be left to individual choice.

It is to be seen that Hindu children go through the training of *Brahmacharya āshramas*. The educational institutions of the day should be remoulded after that pattern. The old ideas and ideals must be infused into them. Spiritual education must be imparted along with the secular.[1] Character-building on spiritual foundations should be the most prominent feature of the entire course of education.

Such training only will enable one to live the

[1] Cf. *Mund. Up.* I. 1.4.

householder's life correctly and, after that, to enter the *Vānaprastha* stage without any pang.

The essential moral discipline, however, has not changed. A person who wants to tread the Path of Desire (*Pravritti Mārga*) must strive to be clean in his thoughts and deeds. Righteous conduct should be his motto. He must practise truth in thought, word and deed. He should preserve cleanliness of the body and mind. He must not injure others. He must not have anything to do with fraud or deceit. And he should not be too much addicted to sense-objects. He should try his best to bring the senses under his control.

Together with this moral discipline, he should perform the *Deva* and *Pitri yajnas* in their current forms and the three other *yajnas* as of old as well as the *varnāshrama* duties, as far as practicable under the present conditions. This, in short, comprises the *dharma* of the modern Hindus who want to take up the *Pravritti Mārga*.

VIII

NIVRITTI MĀRGA

THE PATH OF RENUNCIATION

WHAT man really wants is eternal bliss (*shreyas*). Only he does not know where and how to get it. He mistakes sense-pleasures for pure bliss. This is why he desires the attractive things of this world and the next.

Wealth, progeny, fame and hundreds of other things of this world attract him. He runs after them. He seizes some and enjoys them for a while; some elude his grasp and he feels miserable; while some others remain in his clutches for a time and then suddenly disappear. Such losses hurt him. Then again, as soon as he gains some coveted things, fresh desires crop up and make him restless. He finds to his dismay that the senses cannot be appeased by enjoyment. Rather their craving is increased by the process. So his life becomes a non-stop race after these fleeting pleasures. On this path he never attains contentment. Misery, born of unfulfilled desire and parting with coveted things, dogs him at every step. And this goes on from birth to birth, for he has to face death again and again, though he may not like it.

Even the higher and finer worlds where he gets unalloyed pleasures, do not give him eternal bliss.

There a man of meritorious deeds may go after death and enjoy intense pleasures. But that is only for a time. After that he has to come down and be born again on this earth.[1]

Really, so long as man is driven by desire, neither this world nor the next can bring him eternal bliss. Desire is verily the chain that binds him to *samsāra*.

Yet man is loath to part with desire. The craving for sense-objects dominates him. The camel likes to brcwse on prickly shrubs though these make his mouth bleed. Just so, man gloats over sense-pleasures though these bring him untold miseries through repeated cycles of births and deaths.

The number of such men is very great indeed. For them the first step is to take the *Pravritti Mārga*, that is, the Path of Desire. They are not to give up all desires. Only they have to regulate these by faithfully following the injunctions (*vidhi*) and prohibitions (*nishedha*) of the *Shāstras*. Those who do this enjoy the good things of this world and the next. And their minds become purified to some extent. After enjoying the intense pleasures of the higher worlds they come back to this earth and tread the Path of Desire with more devotion. Again their meritorious deeds lead them to the intense pleasures of the higher worlds after death.

[1] Cf. *Mund. Up.* I. 2. 10.

This process goes on over and over again till their minds become very pure.

At this stage they realize the vanity of desires. By their repeated experience they grasp the truth that desires are never quenched by enjoyment, just as fire can never be quenched by butter. Unfulfilled desires make one unhappy. Moreover, the period of enjoyment even in the higher worlds is limited. By their own observation they become convinced that the Path of Desire cannot lead them to eternal bliss. And it is this eternal bliss that they have been seeking all the time. Realizing the futility of desires, they go out in quest of the path that may lead them to eternal bliss, eternal life and infinite knowledge.[1]

This quest is the very starting-point of real religion. The *Pravritti Mārga* is no more than a preliminary discipline. It serves its purpose by making our minds pure enough to realize the futility of running after sense-objects. This precisely is its scope. It takes us no farther than that on the road to perfection.

So long as we remain pinned to sense-objects for our enjoyment, the Divinity within remains concealed from our view. Our gaze has to be drawn away from the sense-objects and turned inward to realize Him. Then and then only it is possible for us to attain perfection, and get eternal bliss, eternal life and infinite knowledge.

[1] Cf. *ibid.* I. 2. 12.

Our desire for sense-objects is, therefore, the only hurdle on the road to perfection. It makes us world-bound. We have to cross this hurdle. Real religion begins and ends with this crossing. The moment we are free from desire we become divine.

The *Nivritti Mārga*, that is, the Path of Renunciation, leads us to this goal. It teaches us how we may root out our desires and thereby unfold our spiritual nature. This, therefore, is pre-eminently the path of religion.

This is why those who extol the *Pravritti Mārga* too much and consider it to be the supreme religion[1] are denounced by *Bhagavān* Sri Krishna in the *Gitā*.

Indeed, religion begins with the Path of Renunciation. In the *Katha Upanishad* a beautiful *shloka* gives the whole thing in a nutshell: "The Creator has made our senses outward-bound; this is why we (ordinarily) perceive the external world and not the Self. Some poised men, however, desirous of immortality, realize the Self after drawing their senses away from the sense-objects."[2]

Our Upanishads abound with such passages. Take another: "Neither by rituals nor progeny, nor by wealth, but by renunciation alone some attained immortality."[3]

Compare with the above the common saying:

[1] Cf. *Gitā* II. 42.   [2] *Ka. Up.* II. 1. 1.   [3] *Kai. Up.* I. 2.

"Where there is *Rāma* (God), there is no *kāma* (desire); where there is *kāma* (desire), there *Rāma* (God) is not." Sri Rāmakrishna, in our days, put it thus: "If you desire to attain God, you will have to renounce *kāma-kānchana* (lust and possession)."[1]

This is the *Nivritti Mārga*. The path is, no doubt, hard and long. Yet it is the only path to be trod if we want to go ahead towards perfection.

The *Nivritti Mārga*, however, comprehends a number of alternative routes to perfection. The same destination may be reached by train, car, boat or aircraft through different tracks on land, water and air. It is for us to choose the conveyance and the route that will suit our convenience. Similarly, there are various routes within the *Nivritti Mārga* leading to the manifestation of the Divinity within us. It is for us to choose the route that will suit us best.

The different paths prescribed by Hinduism are suited to men of different nature. Some people like action, some prefer contemplation. Some are emotional by nature, some others want to rely more on reason than on emotion. Our religion shows a distinct path to each group.

[1] Swāmi Vivekānanda has made this point clear by saying, "Darkness and light, enjoyment of the world and enjoyment of God, will never go together. 'You cannot serve God and Mammon.' Give up everything for the sake of the Lord."

Even in other religions we notice the same emphasis on renunciation. Christ said to a rich young man, "Give up all that thou hast and follow me." Once he said, "Whosoever will save his life, shall lose it; and whosoever will lose his life for my sake, shall find it."

These paths are called *yogas*. *Yoga* literally means union. These paths lead us to a stage when we become aware of God. Hence they may be said to unite us with God. Of course, the union has all along been there; by *yoga* we become conscious of this fact. However, this is why these paths are called *yogas*.

Broadly speaking, there are four such *yogas* to suit four different types of men. For the men of action there is *Karma-yoga*, for the rationalists *Jnāna-yoga*, for the emotional men *Bhakti-yoga* and for the empiricists *Rāja-yoga*.

In the *Gitā* Sri Krishna says, "Out of thousands of men one strives sincerely for liberation."[1] Indeed, few people want sincerely to rise above nature and be free. Only those who experience, through repeated births, the hollowness of sense-pleasures go in for renunciation. To them only the desire for sense-objects appears to be a bondage, which they want earnestly to break through.

For doing this they have to take up any of the four *yogas* and go through the spiritual discipline prescribed by it. Their *gurus* or spiritual guides show them the paths that suit them best and advise them as to how they may get over the difficulties in the way. Hinduism is very clear about the necessity of a spiritual guide (*guru*) for a spiritual aspirant (*sādhaka*).

[1] *Gitā* VII. 3.

IX

RĀJA-YOGA

THERE are some people who cannot take anything on trust. They want to be convinced of anything only by tangible results. In a word, those with a scientific outlook come within this group. And in these days the number of such people is on the increase.

To such people *Rāja-yoga* is admirably suited. It does not require anybody to swallow any dogma nor to perform any mystifying ritual. It prescribes simply a graded course of mental concentration. And the courses are perfectly rational. The goal of *mukti* is reached when the mind becomes absolutely still.

It is described as *Ashtānga-yoga* because it prescribes eight successive courses through which one has to pass. One need not start with faith in anything. One may even take up the courses, one after another, with the idea of testing their efficacy. If a sincere attempt be made, even the preliminary courses may thrill a novice with novel experience within a short time.

EIGHT COURSES

Yama, niyama, āsana, prānāyāma, pratyāhāra, dhāranā, dhyāna and *samādhi* are the eight successive courses.

The first two are meant for moral purification. *Yama* consists of non-injury, truthfulness, non-stealing, continence (self-control) and non-receiving of any gift. *Niyama* stands for cleanliness, contentment, austerity, study and self-surrender to God. Without these moral assets no spiritual progress is possible. So one must be well-grounded in *yama* and *niyama* before proceeding further.

The next step is *āsana*. This is only a sort of physical exercise. The object is to train the body to sit erect for a long time. Various postures are prescribed. In all of them, however, the spinal column has to be kept erect; the head, neck and chest have to be held in a straight line. One may choose any of these postures and practise it till one can sit motionless for at least an hour.

Prāṇāyāma is a breathing exercise. Rhythmic breathing helps concentration of mind. Sitting still (*āsana*), together with rhythmic breathing (*prāṇāyāma*), makes the mind fit for looking inward. For the practice of *prāṇāyāma* one should be guided by an expert. Else it may vitally injure the body.

The next step is *pratyāhāra*, which means drawing in of the sense-organs. The mind is agitated mightily and ceaselessly by these organs. The eyes, ears, etc. on the physical body are only outer instruments. Corresponding to them there are subtle counterparts which are called *indriyas* (sense-organs) by our *Shāstras*. Normally, these

inner organs remain attached to their respective
outer instruments; and as the latter come in
contact with their objects (*vishaya*), the former
break out into waves of distinct forms and stir
up corresponding waves in the mind. When the
physical eyes, for instance, contact a flower, the
inner organ of sight produces the form of flower
in the mind. And it is this mental form that we
see outside. Thus with all our sensations of colour,
sound, smell, taste and touch. Each sensation
corresponds to a particular modification of the mind
through an *indriya*. Thus so long as one remains
awake, the outer instruments remain in contact
with their objects and go on subjecting the inner
organs of perception (*jnānendriya*) together with the
mind to a non-stop series of modifications (*vritti*).

Yet this is not all. The perceptions brought
about in this way call up, by suggestions, from
within the depths of the mind, allied thoughts
and impulses and stir up the inner organs of work
(*karmendriya*). This is followed immediately by the
formation of waves of will in the mental stuff. I see
a flower; thoughts and impulses rush up from
within the mind and determine a will to seize the
flower. All these are successive changes of the
mental stuff. Hence, as long as the inner organs
remain attached to the outer instruments, the mind
is bound to be in a state of continuous turmoil.

Pratyāthāra consists in detaching the inner organs

(*indriyas*) from the outer instruments and thus keeping them unruffled. This is a great step forward towards pacifying the mind. At first one is advised to control the bubbling up of sub-conscious thoughts. This is done by letting the mind run on and watching the thoughts that come up from within the depths of the mind. This mental exercise is a sort of emptying the mind. It gradually slows down the rush of thoughts from within to the surface of the mind. As this goes on, the mind becomes steadier and along with that the nerves become more and more soothed and strengthened. One can then get a hold on the inner organs and try to detach them from the outer instruments.

With the gradual steadiness of the mind achieved through *pratyāhāra*, all its faculties become keener. The powers of observation, reasoning, and memory will increase as the restlessness of the mind decreases. Really a steady mind is a keen, firm and vigorous mind. Character must have such a mind for its basis. *Pratyāhāra* goes a long way to ensure such steadiness by freeing the mind from a good deal of external and internal disturbance. However, after practising *pratyāhāra* for some time, one feels that the mind has become rather pliable and ready for concentration on one object or idea.

At that stage one should try to fix the mind on a single object. He may choose any object on which he is to meditate. Yet, he will find that, in spite of his best efforts, the mind does not remain glued to his chosen object. The object appears to be hazy and there are breaks in the concentration. But he has to make repeated attempts. This process is called *dhāranā*.

Dhāranā leads naturally to *dhyāna*. Repeated attempts at fixing the mind on one object help one to do that thoroughly for a short stretch of time. The mind then appears to flow in an unbroken current towards its target. This stage of the mind is what is known as *dhyāna*.

Through intense practice *dhyāna* is followed by another step called *samādhi*. This is concentration *par excellence*. During *samādhi* the mind loses its grip on all other things. As in deep sleep, a man in *samādhi* becomes unconscious of everything about him. Even the object of meditation melts away. Yet *samādhi* makes the mind keener than ever. It is in this state that the real import of the object comes like a flash and occupies the entire mind. Then and then alone one's knowledge about the object becomes complete.

This state of the mind is called *samprajnāta samādhi*. By meditating on any object in nature till the mind is merged in such *samādhi*, one can have a thorough knowledge of it. With such deep and direct knowledge comes mastery or complete control over the object. Through such concentration

on the gross *bhutas* (earth, water, fire, air and ether)
the Hindu *yogis* gain the power of controlling
external nature.

The first five steps are only preparations of
yoga, that is, concentration. The last three, namely,
dhāranā, *dhyāna* and *samādhi*, constitute the course of
concentration proper known as *samyama*. *Samyama*
starts with *dhāranā*, which matures in due course
into *dhyāna* and *samādhi*, one after the other.

Samyama is to be practised first on gross objects
and then gradually on finer and finer ones. In the
finer stage, the mind itself becomes the object of
concentration. Through this the Hindu *yogis* gain
control over their own minds as well as over
those of others, and come to know intimately
everything in nature, external and internal.

Yet this is not the goal. *Samprajnāta samādhi*
brings out the latent powers, reveals the secrets
of all objects in external and internal nature and
enables the *yogi* to gain complete control over
them. But it falls short of revealing the divinity
of his Self and liberating him from *samsāra*. A
slip even from such a stage may whirl him through
several births of miserable existence.

But he stands almost at the gate of the Supreme
Realization. If the *yogi* patiently persists in his
practice of *samādhi* on his own mind, at a certain
stage a very wonderful event takes place. Suddenly
the mind becomes perfectly still. This is known as

asamprajñāta samādhi. As soon as this happens, the last cover seems to have been taken off and the Self stands revealed in Its divine glory. The *yogi* then really comes to the very core of his being and realizes it as nothing but God.

When his consciousness comes back to the normal plane, the *yogi* appears to be thoroughly transformed. There is nothing for him to desire, fear or grieve for. He has reached the goal. His heart is full of peace. With love and compassion for all, he goes about guiding others on the path of liberation.

WORDS OF CAUTION

The path of *Rāja-yoga*, however, is full of pitfalls. One should beware of these from the very beginning. Any undue haste is dangerous. The essential moral preparation through the practice of *yama* and *niyama* must be completed before taking up any of the following courses. Otherwise the *yogi*'s toil may just end in wrecking his body. All sorts of physical ailments, reaching up to nervous disorder and even to insanity, may be the result of such rash endeavour. Then, the practice of *prāṇāyāma* without a guide has every chance of proving equally risky. One may with more benefit skip over this step altogether and take up *pratyāhāra*.

With *pratyāhāra*, the mind begins to know itself.

The *yogi* enters a new region and starts getting some novel experience. As his concentration deepens through *dhāranā*, *dhyāna* and *samādhi*, he discovers the immense potency of the mind. Much of the mental energy remains untapped and a good deal is wasted by the ordinary man. *Yoga* enables one to release the latent powers and work wonders with them. These supernormal powers are known as *siddhis*. Hypnotism, telepathy, clairvoyance and clairaudience, and many more miraculous feats may easily be performed by a *yogi* with the help of these *siddhis* (occult powers).

But these powers may just entrap a *yogi*. Like riches, these wonderful powers may divert his mind from the path of God. He may feel tempted to display these for winning wealth and adoration. If he does that, he becomes lost over again in the maze of *samsāra*.

A real seeker of Eternal Bliss should never yield to such temptations. He must never seek such power nor make a show of them when these come to be acquired through the practice of *yoga*.

There are some people, however, who take up *Rāja-yoga* only for the attainment of worldly things and miraculous powers. They want to improve their health, beauty or youth and to impose on others by showing miracles. Evidently these people are selfish and world-bound. Occult powers in their possession are apt to prove dangerous to society.

They may do a lot of mischief to their fellow-men. Thus *Rāja-yoga*, which can help us to manifest our divinity, is liable to be abused by these power-seekers. One should beware of those who interpret *yoga* in terms of temporal powers. Spirituality has nothing to do with these powers. Any desire for these, like all other desires for worldly things, is suicidal to spiritual life and is to be shunned like poison.

X

JNĀNA-YOGA

DIVERS get to the bottom of the sea and fish out pearls. Our Hindu *rishis* were superdivers. Instead of going out to the sea for a dive, they plunged within themselves and found a wonderful treasure, much more valuable than all the wealth of the world. After such a successful plunge one of the *rishis* came out and declared, "Listen, O ye children of the Immortal One, who reside in this world or in the brighter ones, I have known the Great One, knowing whom one goes beyond death (ignorance)."[1] Diving within himself the *rishi* did really reach the bottom of the universe and discover the great treasure that can take us beyond death.

The *rishi* wanted to know himself. Withdrawing his mind from the sense-world, he applied it to make a vigorous search for his real Self. This led him to a point where the mind was hushed into silence and the Self stood revealed in all Its glory. The *rishi* saw who he really was. He discovered that his Self (*Ātman*) was no other than God—the Great Spirit (*Brahman*) within the universe. Thus, realizing his oneness with God, he reached the goal of liberation (*mukti*), and cried 'Eureka!' in the abundance of joy.

[1] *Shwet. Up.* II. 5. & III. 8.

What a miracle! A man becomes God as soon as he knows himself. Well, man is not something other than God. Essentially he is God always. Only he has to discover this fact for himself. And this is all that he has to do for liberation (*mukti*).

The spiritual practice (*sādhanā*) that leads one straight to this discovery is what is known as *Jñāna-yoga*. *Jñāna* means knowledge, and *Jñāna-yoga* stands for concentration on Self-knowledge. Such concentration helps one to penetrate the depths of ignorance (*avidyā*) and realize that the real Self (*Ātman*) is none other than the Great One (*Brahman*).

This *yoga* is based on the *Jñāna-kānda* of the Vedas. The Upanishads dwell mainly on this theme. They enjoin, 'Know thyself.'[1] And why? Because, they declare, 'The real Self of man is verily the same as the Great One.'[2] So, by knowing oneself, one realizes the Great One, and becomes one with Him.[3] He becomes a liberated soul (*mukta purusha*).

These are no empty words or mere dogmas. They are spiritual truths discovered by the *rishis* of the Upanishads. And they have since been verified by thousands of blessed saints and seers of this holy land.

Jñāna-yoga stands on such spiritual truths and throws open a direct approach to Self-knowledge (*Ātma-jñāna*) and hence to liberation (*mukti*).

---

[1] Cf. *Mund. Up.* II. 2. 5.   [2] *Bri. Up.* II. 5. 19.
[3] Cf. *Mund. Up.* III. 2. 9.

It does not prescribe any code of rituals. Nor does it require one, like *Rāja-yoga*, to go through any quasi-mechanical exercise of the body and mind. Cogitations on the essence of one's being as revealed by the *Shāstras*, followed by meditation on the same, are about all that comprise the *Jnāna-yoga* course. And this is precisely why this *yoga* appeals to those intellectuals who are rationalistic by nature.

No detour has to be made by the *Jnāna-yogi*. He cuts across the domain of ignorance (*Avidyā*) with the sword of discrimination (*viveka*) and reaches the goal by the shortest route.

But it is not easy to make such a short-cut. A good deal of mental preparation is necessary before one may take to *Jnāna-yoga*. One must have a very sound and pure mind before going in for this course. The divinity of the Self can be realized only with the help of a very fine and pointed intellect,[1] and the intellect attains such a state only when the mind is thoroughly purified.

This is why only those who are well-grounded in the four requisites (*sādhana-chatushtaya-sampanna*)[2] are said to be qualified for taking up this *yoga*.

He must discriminate between the Real (God) and the unreal (universe). He must not hanker after anything of this world or the next ones. His senses and mind must remain entirely under his control and he must remain contented under all circum-

---

[1] Cf. *Ka. Up.* I. 3. 12.   [2] *Br.* S. I. 1.—*Shankara-Bhāshya.*

stances. He has to put up with all afflictions that may come in his way and that without any grudge or regret. He must have intense faith in himself and in the spiritual truths discovered by the *rishis*. He must have concentration of mind. And, above all, he must have a burning desire for attaining *mukti* and one-pointed devotion to gaining this end.

Without such mental equipment meditation on the Self is impossible. By cogitation about the real nature of the Self one may at best succeed in getting a hazy intellectual conception about It. Any further progress is simply barred. And compared with the realization of the Self, this conception is trash. It may enable one merely to talk glibly on the subject like an erudite scholar (pundit). And that is about all an unclean mind may get on this path. Spiritual illumination is a long way off, attainable only by pure ones.

To persons with the necessary qualifications *Jnāna-yoga* presents only three steps, namely, *shravana* (hearing), *manana* (cogitating) and *nididhyāsana* (meditating).

The first step (*shravana*) consists in hearing about the real Self. One has to do this from an illumined guide. A liberated sage alone can speak effectively on the subject[1] and clear the pupil's doubts, provided the pupil also is duly qualified. Such a sage has to be approached by the pupil with humility,

---

[1] Cf. *Mund. Up.* I. 2. 12.

pertinent queries and service[1] so that he may dis-
close the secrets of Self-knowledge. When, however,
such a sage is not available, one has to be guided at
least by a well-advanced soul. Under such guidance
one should study the relevant Scriptures dealing
with Self-knowledge.

The second step is *manana*, that is, cogitation.
One has to reason out what has been heard from the
guru (spiritual guide) and the *Shāstras* (Scriptures).
A good deal of hard and almost constant thinking
is necessary, since one has to dwell on very subtle
abstractions. And this has to be done with one-
pointed attention. This, in short, is what *manana*
stands for.

Normally, we have a lot of confused thinking,
and this has to be corrected as far as possible by
manana. Although our observation and study enable
us to know a good many things of the universe, it
is a fact, that we know very little about ourselves.

'I', 'me', 'my', 'mine' are the most commonly
used words. I am the subject and the entire world
outside is the object of my experience. The world is
thus divided into myself as the subject of experience
and everything else grouped together as the object
of my experience. Of these two groups, the subject
is surely the more important one. As a matter of
fact, I am the very centre of my view of the world.

In spite of such paramount importance of one's

[1] Cf. *Gitā* IV. 34.

self, we appear to have a very muddled idea about ourselves. Our very talks betray this fact. Indeed it is most surprising to note that we scarcely know what part of our being we precisely refer to by the word 'I'. Yet this word stands for something with which one is most vitally concerned and all other things come after that.

When I say, "This is a horse", I surely mean that the horse is something distinct from me, that it is only an object of my experience. When I say, "This is my horse", I mean that the horse, which is a distinct object of my experience, belongs to me. I never confuse the horse with myself. When the horse kicks, I never say that I am kicking. So far we are perfectly consistent in our thoughts. The same thing holds good whenever we talk of any other object of our experience like the horse.

But when I say, "My body", there is some confusion in my thought. Obviously I mean that the body belongs to me; therefore the body must surely be something distinct from me. It is an object of my experience as much as any other thing. But our ideas are not at all clear on this point. For, when I say, "I am wounded", I betray such confusion. The wound is evidently on the body, which is distinct from myself. But I forget this fact and take the body as myself or as a part of my being when I say, "I am wounded". Thus we say, "I am weak, sick, old", etc. when really the body passes through such states. Even our idea that I am a man or a woman is derived from such confused thinking.

So with the mind. We use the expression 'my mind'. By that surely we mean that the mind is distinct from myself. And do we not witness the functions of our mind just as we observe all external events? Indeed, the mind is an object of our experience like all other things. But we have no clear grasp of this idea. Else how can we say, "I think, I desire, I will", when really the mind is doing all these things? We use both the expressions, 'my mind is worried' and 'I am worried', to convey the same idea. This clearly shows how we are confused about the relation of our mind to ourselves.

The body and mind are distinct objects of my experience. Yet we look upon them as parts of our being. The truth, however, leaks out when we say, "My body", "My mind", etc. Truth and untruth are somehow mixed up in our thought (*Satyanrite mithumkritya*) [1] This, the Hindu *Shāstras* hold, is due to Primal Ignorance (*Avidyā*). This *Avidyā* covers up our real nature and shows us as something that we are not. The selfsame Soul is present in every creature, from the smallest amoeba up to the liberated sage. The difference between them is only in the degree of Its manifestation. As ignorance (*Avidyā*) clears up bit by bit, the Soul becomes more and more manifest.

[1] *Br. S. Shankara-Bhāshya*—Introduction.

On the human plane our ignorance about our real Self is deep enough to make us even think that we are nothing but the body. This is our crudest idea about ourselves. By a little and imperfect discrimination we gradually come to believe that we are the body, the senses and the mind lumped together. When we advance one step farther, we find that the body is only an outer casing, in which we live in a finer state of existence, as a composition of the senses, the mind, intellect (*buddhi*) and vital energy (*prānas*). Proceeding farther, we see that even these are the objects of our experience. We can witness their functioning. At this stage we find that we live in *buddhi* (intellect). Normally that appears to be the seat of all creatures (*jivas*).

Taking his stand on *buddhi*, the *jiva* claims to be the doer of all deeds (*kartā*) and the subject of all experience (*bhoktā*). This is described in one of the Upanishads through a beautiful imagery: 'Know the soul as the rider, the body as the chariot, the *buddhi* as the charioteer, the mind as the reins, the *indriyas* as the horses and the sense-objects as the road they traverse.'[1]

Really we reside as *jivas*[2] in the intellect (*buddhi*), which is a part of the subtle body (*sukshma sharira*) consisting of the intellect, mind, sense-organs and vital energy. As *jivas* we make contact with the gross outer world through the material body (*sthula*

[1] *Ka. Up.* I. 3. 3-4.   [2] See *infra* Chap. XIX.

sharira). Again, leaving the material body alone in light sleep, we become the subject of action and experience in the dream-state as well. With the entire subtle body (*sukshma sharira*) we pass out of the material body at death and enter another at rebirth. Thus as *jivas* we continue living through myriads of births and deaths.

Everyday, however, something very astounding takes place when we fall fast asleep. For, in the state of deep sleep (*sushupti*), we lose all our bearings and simply vanish from the stage, as it were. In that state we do not perceive anything nor can we perform any act. We cease to exist as actors and perceivers. We no longer seem to be *jivas*. We are reduced to the causal state (*kāranāvasthā*). We live with all our thoughts and experiences (*samskāra*) potentially present in this state. And as soon as we are released from *sushupti*, we appear to spring up into existence as the subject of action and perception either on the dream-stage or on the waking one.

Indeed, this phenomenon of *sushupti* is unusual. It causes a break almost everyday in our continued existence as the subject of action and experience. Yet in deep sleep we cannot say that we cease to exist. It is not a total blank or void. We feel that there is a continuity of our existence even through sound sleep. When we wake up, we can say that we had a sound sleep and did not experience anything. On whose evidence do we say that? The active part of our being was not on the stage. Yet there remained something in us that witnessed the sleep-state (*sushupti*). This simple witnessing without any action or experience is, therefore, done by something in us that never goes to sleep. It exists always. And this is precisely our real Self (*Sākshi-chaitanya*). The Self is neither the doer nor the experiencer. It is the constant witness of all actions and experiences of the *jiva* as the latter passes through the three states of waking, dream and deep sleep and goes on and on from birth to birth.

We are really this witnessing Self. The *jiva*, the actor and perceiver (*kartā* and *bhoktā*) in us, is also an object of experience. Beyond the *buddhi*[1] and distinct from it, we exist eternally as pure Spirit. This is our Soul. And the Hindu *Shāstras* declare that the Soul of us all is one All-pervading Existence. It is an infinite ocean of Existence, Knowledge and Bliss. This is verily *Brahman*, the Infinite One, from whom all the worlds, gross and fine, are projected, in whom they exist and into whom they disappear during *Pralaya* (Dissolution).

Yes, our Soul is one and undivided. Our separate *buddhis*, illuminated by the Consciousness of the selfsame Soul, appear as distinct conscious entities.[2] Like so many moons they shine with the light of the same sun, namely, *Brahman*. And this moon of *jiva*

[1] Cf. *Gita* III. 42.   [2] Cf. *Ka. Up.* II. 2. 15.

in us lights up all that we see about us in the gross
or finer worlds.

Through *manana* along these lines the qualified
aspirant (*sādhaka*) is able, in course of time, to grasp
the fact that, detached from the gross and fine
bodies, he stands aloof as the Witness, the Supreme
Self.

The third step, *nididhyāsana*, requires the *Jnāna-
yogi* at this stage to withdraw himself entirely from
all things and concentrate on the idea, 'I am the
Witness'. When such concentration matures, suddenly everything vanishes from the scene and he
finds himself one with the Eternal Spirit. This state
is called *nirvikalpa samādhi*.

Thus, with the help of these three steps, the
Jnāna-yogi peels the universe layer by layer, as it
were, and reaches its very core and comes to be
blessed with the Supreme Realization.

XI

BHAKTI-YOGA

TULSIDĀS, a famous saint of Hindu India and author of the Hindi *Rāmāyana*, was too fond of his wife in his early days. He could not brook her separation even for a day. Once it so happened that she had to go to her father's house for a short visit. But this was too much for Tulsi to stand. It proved impossible for him to stay at home. So on the very day of her departure he followed her and met her in his father-in-law's house. At this his wife remarked, "How passionately attached you are to me! If you could shift this attachment to God, you would realize Him in no time." This remark worked like magic on Tulsi's mind. He turned round and became a passionate lover of God. In the fulness of time he realized Him and helped others to do the same.

In the Hindu legends there are numerous instances of such transformation. Bilwamangal attained Blessedness when his terrible attachment to a public woman was turned towards God.

Now, these instances give a clue to *Bhakti-yoga* or the Path of Love. *Bhakti-yoga* rests on the simple truth that one can realize God by loving Him. Nothing else is required—neither abstract thinking nor any mechanical exercise of the body and mind. Besides, it does not make any unnatural demand.

Most of us are emotional by nature and we are swayed more by love than by any other emotion. We love ourselves; we love our kith and kin; we love our hearth and home. We love our own community, our nation, our race. We love wealth, power and possession. We are ridden by sex-love. Our love for all these determines most of our activities and shapes our conduct. Moreover, it gives us joy and makes life interesting. It throws a sort of charm on the whole world. Without it life becomes intolerable.

No doubt, love is a basic and universal emotion and, as such, a very potent factor of our life. Every other emotion appears to be stirred up by this basic one. Our fear of death, for instance, arises from our love for life. Hatred springs from excessive love for self-interest. Indeed, the noblest as well as the vilest deeds owe their origin to this ruling passion. Selfless love for others is the prime mover of all pious souls. The inspiration for our bravest acts often comes from this source. The mother faces the lion to rescue her beloved child. The soldier dares death for the love of his country. On the other hand, it is love for one's own interests more than anything else that moves the assassin, the tyrant and the exploiter to their dirty jobs. The gangster is goaded to acts of dare-devilry by his love for the near and dear ones. Thus the crowning social virtues as also the darkest antisocial crimes may be prompted equally by love.

Love'is like the lamp that may be made to illumine an altar as well as to set a house on fire. It all depends on the way we use this mighty emotion.

Bhakti-yoga suggests the best possible use that may be made of this emotion. We may utilize it to reach the goal of life—liberation (*mukti*). All that we have to do is to love God intensely, just as we love any other thing on earth. We all know how to love a person or a thing dearly; we are required only to shift the focus away from worldly objects to God. Through this process our emotional nature gets its full play. So we never have to feel out of our elements. Moreover, as love for God develops, attachment to other things gradually melts away. So renunciation becomes easy and natural. Besides, love for God is accompanied by pure joy from the very beginning. This is why *Bhakti-yoga*, that is, the Path of Love, appeals to the majority of mankind. It is, perhaps, the easiest approach and suited to the taste and capacity of most of us.

Yet love for God is not so easy as it seems to be. So long as there is any trace of desire in one's mind for worldly things, one cannot have a very intense yearning for God. To love an object that pleases our senses is one thing, but to love God, whom we neither see nor feel at the beginning, is surely something quite different.

Bhakti-yoga helps us out of this difficulty. It presents a graded course through which a novice may gradually develop intense love for God that leads him straight to liberation.[1]

This supreme one-pointed love for God is called *parā bhakti*. Such love, attended by ecstatic bliss and visions of God, is coveted by many Vaishnavas as the very goal of their spiritual practice (*sādhanā*). Such devotees (*bhaktas*) after realizing God in this life become perfect. After death they retain their subtle body (*sukshma sharira*) and proceed to higher worlds, where they live eternally in the presence of their beloved Lord.

Now, such love for God is not attained in a day. It has to be cultured. One has to pass through a preparatory course of training. And this is called *gauni* (secondary) *bhakti*. Through devoted practice (*sādhanā*) for a long time *gauni bhakti* gradually matures into *parā* (supreme) *bhakti*.

Just like any other *yoga*, Bhakti-yoga also prescribes a course of moral preparation. One must try to control the passions, practise self-restraint and self-denial, truth, honesty, sincerity, non-injury. One must not covet what belongs to others and should do good to all without a thought of return. One must be strong in body and mind and not give way to excessive mirth.

With such moral make-up one should stick to spiritual practice with grit and determination. For,

[1] A little reflection will make it clear that Christianity and Islam teach *Bhakti-yoga* as the only approach to God.

by this practice alone, he has to draw his mind away
from other things and fix it on God. One who proceeds with unflinching devotion succeeds in the
attempt.

The spiritual practice prescribed by *Bhakti-yoga*
consists of constant thinking of God. Such thought
alone purifies the mind, gives it strength and joy and
takes it farther and farther towards supreme love
for God and liberation (*mukti*). In the *Gitā* Sri
Krishna says, "Those who, having offered up all
their work unto Me, with entire reliance on Me,
meditate on Me and worship Me without any
attachment to anything else—them I soon lift up
from the ocean of death and ever-recurring birth,
as their mind is wholly attached to Me."[1] No
doubt it is quite difficult for the mind to think of
God always. Yet every new and determined effort
makes the task easier, provided the aspirant is not
attached to worldly things.[2]

At first the mind may refuse to move in the same
groove. It may be boring to repeat the same
thought in the same way over and over again.
Bhakti-yoga solves this initial difficulty by showing a
variety of ways through which we may think of
God. We may simply repeat His name, we may
chant hymns and prayers, we may worship Him
with offerings, we may meditate on Him or His
power and glory, we may read the Scriptures about

[1] *Gitā* XII. 6–7.   [2] Cf. *ibid.* VI. 35.

Him as also about those blessed ones who received His grace. Thus we may engage our mind variously in the thought of God. This does away with monotony and makes the practice interesting.

Then, the Hindu idea[1] that God has projected the universe out of Himself makes it rather easy for us to think of Him. We are used to think of anything through its form. A formless void cannot be conceived by us. Now, we may look upon the whole universe as God Himself. It will be easier still if we choose any object within creation and look upon it as God. That also is a form through which God has expressed Himself.

Besides the things that we see about us, however, there are various other divine forms assumed by Him as, for instance, *Nārāyana*, *Shiva*, *Ganapati*, *Surya*, *Durgā*, *Kāli*. As a matter of fact, all the deities (*devatās*) being His manifestations, any of them may be looked upon as the Lord Himself and worshipped with equal benefit. The higher the manifestation, the easier it is for us to look upon it as the Lord.

Moreover, the Hindus believe that God incarnates Himself even as man for helping the spiritual evolution of mankind. Rāma and Krishna are two of the prominent Incarnations (*Avatāra*) of God in this land. One may think of any of these *Avatāras* as God and practise devotion to Him.

The Vaishnavas, who are the leading sponsors

[1] See *infra* Chap. XX.

of *Bhakti-yoga*, take either Sri Rāmachandra or
Sri Krishna as their chosen Ideal (*Ishta*). To love
God through a human form is surely the easiest for
us. We may stand in awe and reverence before the
Formless Almighty God or God with an effulgent
divine form. But that is not love. Love is based on
a sense of kinship. When God appears as man,
He really comes very close to us and we may
easily approach Him. We need not strain our
imagination too much to love God through such a
human form.

PRATIKA AND PRATIMĀ

However, *gauni* (preparatory) *bhakti* consists in
a sincere effort for fixing the mind on God through
any of the forms in creation from a blade of grass to
the great Creator *Brahmā*. Each and every one of
these being His manifestation, is nothing but God.
Thus one may worship the sun, the moon or the
sky as God Himself. He may even think of God as
immanent in the sea or in any of the rivers or
mountains or trees. Even a block of stone or a piece
of metal may be regarded by him as a symbol of
God and worshipped with devotion. Thus through
the *Shālagrāma-shilā* or the *Shivalinga* or other such
symbols the Hindus worship the selfsame God. Now,
the sun, the sky and the *Shālagrāma-shilā*—these
little bits of manifestation of the Infinite and
Eternal *Brahman*—help us to focus our mind on

God. The mind cannot embrace the Infinite. It can dwell on the finite and the concrete. This is why it becomes easy for us to think of God through any of His finite and concrete manifestations. These are called *pratikas*[1] (symbols). They represent God. Worship of God through any of these forms is called *pratika upāsanā*.

The divine forms of God are, moreover, represented by images (*pratimā*) or pictures (*pata*). These images are usually made of clay, stone, metal or wood.[2] Through the *pratimā* the Hindu devotee worships God and none else. He does not display his devotion to a block of stone or metal. Whom do we honour when we put a garland round the portrait or the statue of a departed hero? Obviously the piece of paper or the block of stone is not the object of our adoration. They only remind us of the hero to whom we really offer our homage. Similarly, the symbol or the image reminds one of God, whom the Hindus worship. As a matter of fact, after the worship is over the clay images are often immersed in water. The Hindus regard the *pratimā* as what it represents, namely, God, and not as what it is by itself.

However, the symbol (*pratika*) or the image (*pratimā*) being something concrete, helps us to draw

----

[1] The usual symbols of worship are the *Shālagrāma*, the *Shivalinga*, the Ganges, a precious stone, a holy diagram (*yantra*), a holy book, a jar, water or a flower. Cf. *Matri. T.* Chap. XII.

[2] Cf. *Mats. Pr.* Chap. CCLVIII. 20–21.

our minds away from other sense-objects to itself and through it to God. In a way this may be said to be an aid to our spiritual exercise, a sort of kinder-garten schooling. For through this the sincere aspir-ant arrives at a stage where he sees God, touches God, talks with God—when the image, the temple, the rituals and the Scriptures have served their purpose and retired to the background. Forms and ceremonials have their value in helping us on to supreme love for God (*parā bhakti*).

Now, one should remember the fact that the rituals of *gauni* (preparatory) *bhakti* are meant for cleansing the mind and developing pure and in-tense love for God. We must not confuse this with the selfsame rituals, such as repetition of God's names, hymns, prayers and worship performed by the followers of the Path of Desire. The latter do all these either through fear of punishment for their evil deeds or through a desire for intense sense-enjoyment. They want something of the sense-world in exchange for their worship. Love cannot grow out of such bargaining. Such rituals are only meritorious acts which can bring only the coveted things. These can never lead to supreme love or liberation. Only those who have seen the hollow-ness of sense-enjoyment, and are willing to tread the Path of Renunciation, are fit for taking up any of the *yogas* as the final course of *sādhanā*. So from the very beginning the *Bhakti-yogi* must not pray to God for this or that worldly thing. He should try earnestly to develop disinterested love for Him.

He should place himself under the guidance of a liberated sage who can transmit spirituality to him. The preceptor (*guru*) chooses for him his *Ishta* (chosen Ideal), that is, the form of God best suited to him. And corresponding to each divine form there is a sound-symbol (*mantra*). The *guru* imparts to him the suitable *mantra* that he should repeat everyday with devotion. The *guru* also teaches him how he is to worship his chosen Ideal (*Ishta*). Thus learning the entire preparatory course of *Bhakti-yoga* from his spiritual guide, he is to practise it with earnest devotion from day to day.

Ishta-nishthā, that is, devotion to the selfsame chosen Ideal, is a necessity. One has to stick to the same form of God as his chosen Ideal (*Ishta*). Hanumānji, the great devotee (*bhakta*) of Sri Rāmachandra, said:

"*Shrināthe Jānakināthe abhedah paramātmani*
Tathāpi mama sarvaswah Rāmah kamalalochanah."

'I know that the Lord of Lakshmi and the Lord of *Jānaki* (Sitā) are one as the Supreme Spirit (*Paramātman*), yet my all is in the lotus-eyed Rāmachandra.' This is *Ishta-nishthā*. Without such an unflinching devotion to one's own chosen Ideal, the aspirant cannot make any progress.

In short, worship of the chosen Ideal with un-

flinching devotion is the main course for the novice.
For ensuring better effect it is to be supplemented
by certain other practices. For instance, along with
it the devotee is to sing the Lord's name, listen to
or read *bhakti* Scriptures, resort to or live in holy
places specially associated with his chosen Ideal
and always seek the company of spiritually advanced souls. Above all, he should try earnestly to
resign himself entirely to the Lord. All these are
recommended as aids to the principal course for
maturing his love for God.[1]

Through such practice of preparatory (*gauni* or
vaidhi) *bhakti* the mind becomes purer and begins
to develop love for God. Now, love for God becomes
easier if we can make it flow through any of our
familiar channels. We know the child's love for the
parents, the faithful servant's love for the master;
we know what a real friend's love means; the
mother's love for her children and the faithful wife's
love for her husband are also familiar to us. These
are different attitudes through which one bears and
expresses love towards another. This is why *Bhakti-
yoga* teaches one at this stage to take up any of
these attitudes (*bhāva*) in relation to one's chosen
Ideal (*Ishta*). One may look upon the chosen Ideal
as one's parent, master, friend, child or lover and
try to behave and develop love accordingly.

The *Tāntrika* devotees regard their chosen Ideal

---

[1] Cf. *Ch. Chmta.* II. 22.

as their mother.[1] The Vaishnava cult prescribes five different attitudes, namely, *shānta, dāsya, sakhya, vātsalya* and *madhura*. Of these, the first does not express any personal relationship with the chosen Ideal. One-pointed devotion to Him without any other craving as well as knowledge of His essential nature brings about a calm pose which is called *shānta bhāva*. The seven sages headed by Sanaka are exemplars of this type of devotees. The *dāsya* votary looks upon himself and behaves as the privileged servant of the Lord of infinite glories. Mahāvira is the shining model of this group. *Sakhya, vātsalya* and *madhura* stand respectively for the attitudes of a comrade, a parent and a lady-love assumed by different devotees towards their chosen Ideals. Sri-dāma and the other cow-boys of Vrindāvan as well as Bhima and Arjuna of Hastināpur typify the *sakhya* mood; Yashodā and the milk-maids of Vrindāvan exhibit ideal patterns of *vātsalya* and *madhura* moods respectively.[2]

The five different attitudes of the Vaishnava school differ from one another not only in kind but also in intensity of feeling. As a matter fact the series has been arranged in order of the increasing intensity of love aroused by the different attitudes.[3] *Shānta bhāva* stands for a kind of dispassionate attachment to the chosen Ideal. *Dāsya* is a step

[1] It is interesting to note that the Christians regard God as their Heavenly Father.
[2] Cf. *Ch. Chmta.* II. 19.   [3] *Ibid.*

ahead representing a faithful servant's personal love
and devotion mixed with awe and reverence. The
shāntā votary is awe-struck by contemplating the
essential nature of God, and the *dāsya* votary by
contemplating the infinite glories of Personal God.
Both keep themselves at a respectful distance from
the Lord. The three succeeding attitudes bring the
devotees within a more intimate circle, closer and
closer to the chosen Ideal. Consciousness of the
might and glories of the Lord recedes to the background and He becomes intensely personal. In
sakhya there is actually a sense of equality as between
two comrades. This surely is a very advanced state
of love. In *vātsalya* one looks upon Him as one's
child. In her mad love for Krishna, Yashodā
sincerely believes that the Lord will go hungry if
she does not feed Him. She does not care to think
of Him as the Eternal and Omnipotent one. Indeed,
love through *vātsalya* reaches a frenzied state. The
culmination, however, is reached in *madhura bhāva*,
where the lover and the beloved become one
through the extreme intensity of love. This is typified by Rādhā's love for Krishna. Mirābāi has left a
brilliant record in Hindu history of such love.

When love for God cultured in this way matures
into *parā bhakti*, one reaches the acme of bliss. Verily
then he attains God, who is the very core of
beauty, joy and love. '*Raso vai sah*'[1]—He is the very

[1] *Tait. Up.* II. 7.

essence of bliss. The Hindus do not think that, seated somewhere in heaven in awful majesty, God simply deals out reward and punishment to the virtuous and the sinner. The Hindu idea of Personal God is quite different. His God is nearer than the nearest, dearer than the dearest. The overflowing affection of the mother for her child is no match for God's love for His devotees. The beauty on the face of any charming thing on earth is only a very faint reflection of His divine beauty. '*Tasya bhāsā sarvami-dam vibhāti*'[1]—He shining, everything else shines. His presence cannot strike awe or terror, it thrills one with ecstatic joy. And the bliss is so intense that the devotees (*bhaktas*) want to enjoy it for ever instead of going in for liberation (*mukti*). They crave to enjoy the infinite beauty and infinite joy of Personal God and not to lose themselves in the Impersonal (*Brahman*). They like, as they say, to taste sugar and not to become sugar.

In such a state the devotee sees his chosen Ideal (*Ishta*) all about him as well as in the innermost recess of his own being. To him the whole world becomes an object of love and worship. Even in the tiger and the serpent he sees his Beloved. Such blessed souls radiate love, purity and joy wherever they go, and inspire all who come in contact with them with an urge for spiritual growth.

[1] *Ka. Up.* II. 2. 15.

XII

BHAKTI-YOGA (*continued*)

TĀNTRIKA SĀDHANĀ

A distinct course of spiritual discipline known as *Tāntrika sādhanā* also comes within the scope of *Bhakti-yoga* as much as Vaishnavism.

This course is equally comprehensive and covers the entire ground of spiritual endeavour. It is a wonderful combination of *jnāna, yoga (Rāja-yoga), bhakti* and *karma*, and is suited to men of all stages of spiritual growth. Taking its stand on the essential oneness of the human soul with the Absolute (*Paramātman*), it leads the devotee step by step through concrete forms and rituals to the realization of the Ultimate Truth and resultant liberation (*mukti*).

Different spiritual exercises are prescribed by the Tantras for different groups of devotees. Some are meant for those who are at the lowest rung of the spiritual ladder, so to speak. These people are *tāmasika*, that is, dull, ignorant and lazy by nature and are almost on the brute level. The course prescribed for the edification of this group is called *pashwāchāra* (code of conduct for the brute-man). Some other course of spiritual exercise is prescribed for those who are in the middle, who are *rājasika*, that is, energetic and ambitious by nature. This course is known as *virāchāra* (code of conduct for the heroic souls).

Both these groups very often take up *Tāntrika sādhanā* for acquiring power and satisfying their craving for sense-enjoyment here or hereafter. So, to them *Tāntrika sādhanā* serves only as *Pravritti Mārga* (Path of Desire). As a matter of fact, the Vedic *Deva-yajna* of *Pravritti Mārga* has come to be replaced in our days mostly by *Tāntrika* worship. Like *Rāja-yoga*, *Tāntrika sādhanā* also brings various powers (*siddhis*) to those who go in for these. However, the *Tāntrika sādhanā* for these seekers of power and sense-enjoyment does not come under *Bhakti-yoga*, which is an approach to Divinity through pure, intense and selfless love for God.

There is yet another group of men who may be said to be very near the top rung of the spiritual ladder. These are the men of renunciation. They are *sāttwika* by nature, that is, they possess calmness, purity, contentment and clear vision. The vanity of sense-enjoyment is obvious to these people and they yearn only for realizing God and becoming perfect. For this group the Tantras prescribe the distinct course known as *divyāchāra* (code of conduct for the godly ones). The special feature of this course is that it has to be practised not for gaining anything material, but for realizing God through love. Such *Tāntrika sādhanā*, therefore, comes under *Bhakti-yoga*.

There are as many as sixty-four prominent Tantra texts. And they prescribe hundreds of distinct rituals and ceremonies meant for the three different groups of devotees. Yet some common threads of unity run through all these.

The Tantras hold up the *Shakti* (Divine Energy) aspect of God for worship. And usually *Shakti* is represented in the form of one or other of goddesses like *Durgā, Chandi, Kāli, Bhuvaneshwari, Jagaddhātri*. The *Shakti*-worshippers are known as Shāktas, just as the worshippers of *Vishnu* are known as Vaishnavas. The Shāktas regard their chosen goddess as the Divine Mother.

The Divine Mother conceived through any of the divine forms is really the Creator, Sustainer and Destroyer of this universe. She has no beginning or end. She is Eternal. Space cannot limit Her. She is Infinite and All-pervading. She is All-consciousness. So She is called *Chaitanyamayi*. Creation is Her sport, and so also is Dissolution (*Pralaya*). Hence She is called *Lilāmayi*. She has three distinct phases of Divine Energy, namely, *sāttwika, rājasika* and *tāmasika*. And this is why She is said to be *Trigunamayi*. Through the *tāmasika* phase She appears as insentient matter. Through the *rājasika* She appears as material as well as vital energy (*prāna*) bringing about all sorts of changes in the material world as also in the physical bodies of all creatures. While through Her *sāttwika* phase She appears as the mind in its different functions and poses as the subject of experience and action in each creature. Really She expresses Herself through all the ever-changing names and forms that we call the world. In fact, She is the Power of Becoming, released somehow out of the Eternal and Changeless Being, the *Nirākāra Nirguna Brahman.*

This, indeed, is the Hindu conception of Personal God, who obviously, has no sex. Yet Personal God assumes a male or female form to suit the devotee's approach. The Vaishnavas, the Sauras and the Gānapatyas prefer the male aspect, while the Shāktas choose to look upon Personal God as their Divine Mother. The motherhood of God, no doubt, establishes a very sweet relation between the Deity and the devotee. Like a child the devotee resigns himself to the affectionate love and fostering care of the Divine Mother.

Then, another feature of the *Tāntrika* rituals is that they remind one of the identity of the human soul (*jivātman*) with the Absolute (*Paramātman*), and also of *Shakti* (Divine Energy) as an emanation from the Great One expressing Herself through all forms, all names and all changes. Before proceeding to worship the Divine Mother, the *sādhaka* is required to imagine for some time that his own soul has merged in the Absolute (*Paramātman*), and everything in creation has vanished altogether. Then he is to imagine that out of the Formless

Being has sprung up afresh his own self as the worshipper as well as the Goddess whom he is to worship. Into a clay image of the Goddess he has to breathe life (*prāna-pratishthā*) by making a symbolic contact of his own Divine Soul with it. It is only after this that the image is considered to become a living emblem of the Goddess, when offerings by way of worship are presented to Her.[1]

This clearly shows how the Tantras help us gradually to grasp, through concrete forms, the great Vedāntic Truth, namely, the divinity of our soul. It may be said to be a sort of laboratory work or rather kindergarten schooling for the comprehension of the great Ultimate Truth, through which comes liberation (*mukti*). What the *Jnāna-yogi* strives to arrive at purely by discrimination and abstract contemplation, the *Tāntrika sādhaka* tries to reach through his course of rituals.

Another common element of the Tantras is the emphasis laid by them on the repetition of certain word-symbols (like *hrim*, *krim*, etc.). Each of these stands for a particular aspect of God expressed through a particular form. No doubt, through every form God is regarded as the Creator, Sustainer and Destroyer of the universe. Yet through the different forms God appears as different Personalities, as it were, with different groups of prominent qualities. Thus *Kāli*, *Tārā*, *Shodashi*, *Chandi*, *Durgā*, *Jagad-*

---

[1] See *infra* Chap. XX.

dhātri—each has a distinct form and a distinct group of attributes, and corresponding to each there is a distinct name as well as a word-symbol. By the repetition of this word-symbol (*mantra*) as directed by the Tantras, one's mind becomes purified and one gets closer and closer to one's chosen Ideal (*Ishta*). Such repetition is usually conjoined with meditation of the form-symbol, for that is more effective.

Then there is another common feature of the *Tāntrika* rituals and in this the Tantras differ widely from *Jnāna-yoga*. While the latter wants its followers to avoid temptations, the Tantras direct their votaries to face these boldly and overcome them. Some of the *Tāntrika* rites require a votary to make contact with attractive sense-objects and at the same time to draw his mind away from such things and fix it on contemplation of his chosen Goddess. He is required to sublimate by this process his sense-attraction into pure love of God. For instance, contact with wine or woman is a feature of some of the *Tāntrika* rites. But then, wine is not meant for intoxication, nor woman for gratification. The votary is to resist the vigorous pull of these lures and concentrate his mind on his chosen Ideal. This is a daring method, no doubt; but if it is successfully followed, one conquers flesh by one stroke, as it were.

Yet it is for this feature that the Tantras have

acquired a bad name. The approach of the Tantras, however, deserves no censure. The Hindus believe that the goal of liberation is reached when one realizes God, and this realization is had only when one's mind is completely concentrated on God. This is what all the *yogas* take their stand upon. And it is towards this end that the Tantras only propose a peculiar technique of their own.

This technique consists simply in utilizing the universal overwhelming emotions that naturally draw our minds away from all other directions and make them one-pointed. A strong sex-appeal or fear of imminent death, for instance, may do the same. Now, exposing the votary to either of these overwhelming emotions means converging his thoughts to one point. The mind is thus focussed on a sense-object through a surging emotion. And then instead of allowing him to go any farther along the line, the Tantras direct him to turn his already focussed mind towards God. The task becomes easy by this process. It is like focussing an astronomical telescope on a distant terrestrial object as a sort of rough adjustment.

This is why some of the *Tāntrika* rites require the votaries to meditate on God after pitching up the sex-impulse through contact with wine or woman. This is also why some other rites require the devotees to fix their minds on God while seated in the midst of the most dreadful surroundings. They are directed, for instance, to sit on a corpse in a lonely crematorium on the darkest night of a month.

Such device of the Tantras makes for a swift march to the goal, no doubt. Yet it is full of risks for the unwary. Particularly, a man of renunciation must be very cautious if he happens to choose this path. Any weakness of the flesh may just make him yield to the passions worked up by the requirements of the daring rites. And in that case, all his efforts for the realization of God will end inevitably in a crash, physical as well as mental.

Many have attained Blessedness through *Tāntrika sādhanā*. Rāmaprasāda and Bāmā Kshepā are familiar names in Bengal. Sri Rāmakrishna in our days has verified the truth of this branch of the Hindu *Shāstras* by his own realizations when he went through its prescribed rites.

NIRĀKĀRA UPĀSANĀ

Hinduism also prescribes devotion to Personal God without any form (*Saguna Nirākāra Brahman*). There are many among the intellectuals to whom God with a form does not appeal.

Yet one should be cautious before banishing forms from spiritual practice. It is really not so easy as it may appear to be. A man with a gigantic intellect may after all be no more than a baby in the spiritual school. He may just require some kindergarten exercise.

Moreover, the findings of our intellect on things spiritual cannot be a safe guide. Our intellect may assert that Infinite God cannot have a finite form. Hinduism also admits that *Parabrahman* is Formless (*Nirākāra*). It even goes further and holds that It has no qualities either. For do not all contradictory qualities like good and evil, kindness and cruelty, hardness and softness, come out of that one undivided Existence? How can the Absolute *Brahman* be limited by any group of qualities to the exclusion of others? Yet Hinduism teaches the truth that this *Brahman* without form and without qualities is the only source of creation.[1] Somehow this eternally Changeless *Brahman* becomes, or rather appears as the universe as well as its Ruler, the Personal God. This is His *Māyā*.

Now, *Nirguna Brahman*, which by inscrutable *Māyā* can express Itself through all the names and forms of the universe, can very well appear in the garb of any divine form. Who is there to limit Its capability? Our intellect is too poor a thing after all to give a ruling in this matter.

Then again, how do we conceive Infinite God as our Heavenly Father listening to our prayers and dealing out justice and showering mercy? How does our intellect sanction such narrowing down of the Absolute? The Absolute cannot be limited either by form or by qualities. It is Transcendental,

[1] Cf. *Br. S.* I. 1. 2.

beyond the range of human thought and speech.[1] None can worship such *Brahman*. Yet to turn our mind Godward we try to conceive Him through a group of qualities and call Him Merciful and all that. This facilitates our approach to Divinity. If we can do this much for the facility of our *sādhanā* (spiritual practice), on precisely the same ground, there is no harm in meditating on God through any of the prescribed forms. Rather, this would make it easier for us to fix the mind on God.

Indeed, our mind is so constituted that it cannot grasp an abstraction. It requires something concrete to hold on to. And this is why even those who are up against forms of God cannot do away with forms altogether in their spiritual practice. The very conception of the Heavenly Father, the very reference to God by the pronouns 'He' or 'She', the very description of His or Her abode in heaven, all these together with the particular structures of our places of worship, as well as all details of rituals, rest entirely on concrete forms.

All these have to be considered and weighed carefully before dispensing with worship of God through symbols (*pratikas*) and images (*pratimās*). Mere intellectual snobbery may lead to sophistry, ending perhaps in materialism. We should beware of this. Only those who in their spiritual practice have outgrown the necessity of such aids as

[1] Cf. *Tait. Up.* II. 9. 1.

symbols or images offer, may go in for *saguna nirākāra upāsanā.*

Such devotees are advised to meditate on the all-pervading presence of God. Certain appropriate imageries are suggested by our *Shāstras* through which such contemplation becomes easier. One may consider oneself to be like a fish in the ocean surrounded on all sides by water and replace the water by God. One may contemplate that just as an empty jar is filled and surrounded by air or ether, so is one by God. Such devotees also have suitable hymns, prayers and modes of worship prescribed by the Hindu *Shāstras.* If those who are really fit for choosing this path persist in their spiritual practice with sincere love for God, they also are sure to reach the goal just like any other *Bhakti-yogi.*

The spiritual history of the Hindus is replete with countless instances of blessed seers of Truth (*siddha mahāpurushas*) from among the adherents of every school of *Bhakti-yoga.*

XIII
KARMA-YOGA

BHAGAVĀN Sri Krishna pulled up the chariot on the battle-field of Kurukshetra just on the eve of the great Kuru-Pāndava war, so that Arjuna, the outstanding Pāndava hero, might review the opposing armies. Seated on the chariot, Arjuna looked round and saw before him his own kinsmen arrayed on both sides and ready to plunge into a deadly fight.

He was very much moved by this sight. The idea of killing his near, dear and respected ones in the battle was shocking. How could he take part in such a heinous affair? Blinded by greed and jealousy, the opposite party might rush into it. But it was certainly not for him to have anything to do with such an inhuman job. No, not for victory and recovery of their lost kingdom, nor even for the mastery of heaven, could he be tempted into it. He could not, for anything in heaven and earth, stoop so low as to have a hand in such an ignoble act. His whole system revolted against the idea of fighting his own kinsmen. Becoming thoroughly upset by such thoughts, Arjuna refused to fight, and asked his Divine Charioteer to turn round.

Sri Krishna, however, did not let him have it as he desired. Instead, he rather charged Arjuna for giving himself up to a spell of mental weakness. He pointed out that Arjuna was under a delusion. He had confounded mere emotionalism with spirituality. As a cultured Aryan he ought to have known better. His behaviour was unworthy of himself. It would soil his fame as a great hero and also bar his entry into heaven. It was a righteous war which, as a Kshatriya, it was his clear duty to fight. His religion required it. He was to follow the Kshatriya code of duties enjoined by the *Shāstras*. It was not for him to leave that and retire to the forest like the Brāhmins.

At this, Arjuna became more confused. He could not reconcile himself to the obviously cruel and immoral deed. He told Sri Krishna plainly that he was not a seeker of anything here or hereafter. Neither fame nor even heaven had any charm for him. Loyalty of *Kshātra-dharma* (code of duties for the warrior class) might bring him only these; but he had no craving for such paltry things. All that he cared for was perfection (*shreyas*). Now, could the slaughter of his own beloved kinsmen and respected teachers fit in with a purely spiritual aim of life? Was there no contradiction between such an atrocious deed and spiritual progress? That was precisely his problem. Unless this was solved, it would not be possible for him to work himself up into a mood to fight. He, therefore, appealed very earnestly to his Divine Friend and Charioteer,

Bhagavān Sri Krishna, to help him out of his dilemma.

Shrimad-Bhagavad-Gitā, the most popular scriptural text of the Hindus, open with this scene. It then proceeds to show how Sri Krishna solved Arjuna's problem by a brilliant discourse on the great spiritual truths discovered by the Vedic *rishis*.

In this discourse it has been made very clear that even a householder can take to the final course of spiritual practice (*Nivritti Mārga*), and this without having to give up his hearth and home. He can live in the midst of a worldly life, attend to all his prescribed duties and yet proceed straight to the goal of Perfection and Blessedness (*shreyas*). No duty, however repugnant, can stand in the path of his spiritual unfoldment. It is the attitude that counts and not the nature of the work one has to do. There is a way of living in the world and doing things that goes to cleanse one's mind thoroughly and make for the highest spiritual achievement.

This way is what is known as *Karma-yoga*. And this is the central theme of Sri Krishna's brilliant discourse recorded in the *Gitā*. As pointed out by Him, this *yoga* had been known to the ancient sages. In course of a long stretch of time, however, people came to forget its use. And this was quite natural. For people are apt to miss the great truth that bridges the gulf between the secular and the spiritual. However, after a long period of lapse,

Sri Krishna restored this *yoga* as a distinct path of liberation.

While appreciating all other approaches to the goal and explaining some of the most important ones like *Jnāna-yoga* and *Bhakti-yoga*, Sri Krishna laid special emphasis on *Karma-yoga*. He portrayed in detail all that it stood for, and elucidated its rationale. For it was this *Karma-yoga* that could solve Arjuna's problem. Even the abhorrent duty of fighting his own kinsmen, which he wanted to avoid, could be turned into the intense and effective spiritual practice of a *Karma-yogi*.

Indeed, *Karma-yoga* is a contrivance through which even a secular duty may be turned into worship (*Yogah karmasu kaushalam*).[1] It is a process of changing the very nature of *karma* (work). Usually, a work brings, as its sure effect (*karma-phala*), either pain or pleasure in this life or the next ones. Thus each work performed by us adds a link to our bondage of *samsāra* (repeated births). This is the rigorous law of *karma*, and normally we have no escape from this. This production of *karma-phala* is an essential feature of *karma*. But through the contrivance of *Karma-yoga* this essential feature is wiped out. *Karma* becomes barren. Instead of adding a link to our bondage, the same work done through *yoga* makes for our release (*mukti*). The work is transformed essentially into spiritual practice.

[1] *Gitā* II. 50.

Now, what is this *yoga* that can bring about such a miracle? *Yoga* is defined in the *Gita* as sameness of mind under all circumstances, that is, equanimity (*Samatwam yoga uchyate*).[1] This *yoga* requires that while doing a work one's mind must not be tossed by any desire for its result. Duty for duty's sake is the formula. Profit or loss, triumph or defeat (*labhalabhau jayajayau*)[2], whatever be the result, it has to be received with equal grace. Such a balanced pose of the mind is called *yoga*. And when with such a mental poise one performs all one's duties, one is said to be a *Karma-yogi*.

Let us look into its rationale. The Vedic religion takes its stand on the unity of existence in God and hence on the divinity and immortality of the real Self of man (Soul). *Brahman* alone exists. We, however, have the illusion of myriads of distinct objects, animate and inanimate, constituting this universe. In our illusion we believe that we are the real and distinct subjects of action and experience, while all these are really done by *Prakriti* (Cosmic Energy).[3] We are under a spell of God's Divine *Maya*, which is very difficult to break through.[4]

So long as we are *Maya*-ridden, so long as we see many and not one, we have, of course, to shape our conduct accordingly. If I feel pain, I should take care not to give pain to others. Thus we have

[1] *Ibid.* II. 48.
[3] Cf. *ibid.* III. 27.
[2] *Ibid.* II. 38.
[4] Cf. *ibid.* VII. 14.

to distinguish between good and evil deeds. But we should know that all these distinctions have only relative values. For the highest view-point, according to the Vedic Religion (Hinduism), there is no such distinction, *Prakriti* (Cosmic Energy) being the agent of all acts.

As a matter of fact, those who reach the highest state look at this world from an altogether different angle. They really see the Great One in and through all, and their own self as none other than the Great One. They realize the true meaning of the creation and enjoy it as a play of the Divine Will. Behind pain and pleasure, health and sickness, life and death, fame and censure, in fact, behind all things, good and evil, they discern nothing but a Divine sport. Centred securely in their real Self, they look upon everything as a manifestation of Divinity. Even virtue and vice lose their distinction with the dawning of real Self-knowledge. The Self neither acts nor experiences. Nor does It undergo any change whatsoever. How can It kill anybody or be killed by anyone?[1]

With such a vision of things the wise ones become self-poised. The Self is Perfection Itself. Hence to those who realize the Self nothing remains to be achieved. No desire for anything can ruffle their mind for a moment. Freed absolutely from mental cravings, these sages remain immersed in Eternal

[1] Cf. *ibid*. II. 19.

Bliss,[1] which is the very nature of the Self. Without any attachment, fear or anger, they covet no pleasure, nor are they afflicted by any sorrow. They receive with equal calmness whatever comes their way, good or evil. They neither hail the one with joy nor curse the other. Their minds rest in perfect peace and equanimity.

Such unique behaviour of the wise ones proceeds naturally from their vision of the great truth about the real Self and the universe. The vision is linked causally with such conduct. Copying such conduct, therefore, as a pattern with sincerity leads one to the great vision and hence to liberation. Herein lies the rationale of *Karma-yoga*. Like the wise ones, one has to strive incessantly to keep the mind in perfect balance under all conditions, and this in the midst of worldly life with all its ties of relationship and demands of duty. 'Eternal calmness in the midst of intense activity' is the ideal condition to be reached. This is *Karma-yoga*.

Karma-yoga, therefore, has two factors, namely, activity and equanimity. One must be intensely active and yet remain calm and self-poised. On the face of it this appears to be an impossible task. How can calmness of mind be preserved when one remains actively engaged in work? Contemplation, meditation, prayer, worship and all that, may be congenial to mental calm. One can understand this.

[1] Cf. *ibid.* II. 55.

But attending to one's secular duties is a different thing altogether. Will it not go to distract the mind and throw it off the balance? No, it cannot. For it is not activity by itself that disturbs the mental calm. Each work rather requires concentration of the mind. It, therefore, offers an opportunity for training the mind in concentration and calmness. Our mind is tossed not by the work itself, but by something else. And that is our desire for the result of our action. We seek these, and that alone makes our mind restless. If we cease to seek the fruits of our action, no amount of activity will ever be able to throw our mind in turmoil. Rather, under such condition, each act will help us on towards mental calmness, purity and clarity of vision till we realize the great truth about ourselves and the world and become free for ever.

Normally, we work because we want something. It is the desire for the fruit that leads us to sow the seeds of action, as it were. Now, if we give up the desire, what will move us to action? Shall we not lapse into inertia (*tamas*)? No. *Karma-yoga* prescribes vigilant attention to one's duties without any desire for their results, and this as a spiritual exercise. It will speed up our march to the goal of Perfection and Blessedness. So our eagerness for spiritual progress will be the incentive to our work. Activity reduces lethargy (*tamas*), and striving to root out desires subdues restlessness (*rajas*). And the reduction of these two goes to increase calmness, purity and clarity of vision (*sattwa*). Thus does *Karma-yoga* purify the mind and help the dawning of Self-knowledge.

Such purification of the mind (*chitta-shuddhi*) through *Karma-yoga* till it rests in equanimity is declared by the *Gitā* to be a necessary course for all spiritual aspirants (*Ārurukshormuneryogam karma kāranam uchyate*).[1] One may, if one so chooses, break off social ties only after such a state of mind is attained. For then and then alone it is possible for such a mind to remain immersed in God-consciousness. Of course, it is possible for even such a one to remain in the world as a householder and work for its well-being, like Janaka and other sages. However, before embracing *Sannyāsa* (life free from worldly obligation) and plunging in any kind of spiritual practice, one is advised by the *Gitā* to attain equanimity (*yoga*) through *Karma-yoga*. Without such mental preparation, renunciation of all worldly ties and duties instead of making for spiritual progress brings one to grief (*Sannyāsastu mahābāho duhkhamāptum ayogatah*).[2]

Yet it must be said that *Karma-yoga* is not so easy as it appears to be. To give up all desires for the results of our action is not a simple affair. Even when the senses are brought under control and the grosser desires are subdued, the finer and stronger

[1] *Ibid.* VI. 3.　　　　[2] *Ibid.* V. 6.

ones like those for name, fame, status, honour, etc. prove very hard nuts to crack. They give a very tough fight. Often it is difficult even to detect their presence. They remain hidden in the subconscious depths of the mind. And this makes the task almost impossible.

There is, however, a way of tackling this task. We are advised to work at the source of our desires. What does give rise to the desires? That has to be found out and stopped. Our senses are naturally attracted by certain things and repelled by others.[1] When the mind is allowed to run after the senses, it gets attached to the former group and starts hating the latter. And this attachment and hatred breed all our desires. We want to seize the attractive objects and avoid the repulsive ones. So, to root out our desires we have somehow to get over these primary feelings of attachment and repulsion towards all worldly objects.

This may be done by a sheer force of will. A determined effort to look alike upon friend and foe, success and failure, profit and loss, health and illness and all the 'dual throng', is all that is necessary. While striving hard to maintain such a mental poise, one must attend to one's duties with all the skill and energy at one's command. This is *Karma-yoga per se*. If pursued earnestly, it is sure to lead one to the spiritual goal as much as any other *yoga*.

[1] Cf. *ibid.* III. 34.

But this process requires a gigantic will, which is rarely to be found. It becomes easier, and hence feasible for many, if it be applied with either *jnāna* or *bhakti*. The sameness of vision towards the pairs of opposites may be acquired through contemplation of God either as the Self or as the Beloved Lord of the universe.

Our attachment and hatred towards the things of the world are rooted in ignorance. We see many in place of the Great One whom the sages realize in and through everything. In our ignorance we feel as if we were separate individuals endowed with bodies and minds. We think that we are the subjects of all actions and experiences. And we start with marking out 'me' and 'mine' from the rest of creation, and valuing them more than anything else. Each one of us takes his stand on such a narrow and unreal view of the Self, and looks upon this unreal self as the centre of the universe. All that appear to cater for the demands of the untrained mind and senses are valued by this little unreal self. Attachment to these and hatred towards the opposite follow and give rise to the never-ending stream of desires. Hence, for giving up desires the *Karma-yogi* should do well to tackle *avidyā* (ignorance). And this is to be done by contemplation of the real nature of the self and the world.

A seeker of Blessedness is advised, therefore, to

take his stand on the higher spiritual plane. He should constantly try to remember the great truth of Divine Unity. He is to consider himself something other than the gross and subtle bodies. He is the Divine Self, standing apart, in peace and tranquillity as the Eternal Witness of all phenomena. He is not the subject of either action or experience. The body, mind, senses, vital energy, intellect (*buddhi*) and ego are all wrought by the Cosmic Energy (*Prakriti*) and worked by her. She is really the subject of all actions and all experiences. So when the body and mind are engaged in any work, one should try to grasp the fact that it is *Prakriti* that is having her way and that the real Self is neither the doer (*kartā*), nor the experiencer (*bhoktā*). The successful *yogi* really feels that he is the unmoved and changeless witness of all that goes on in the body and mind while they are at work or rest, in the waking, dreaming or even sleeping state. He never feels that he is doing anything even when work is performed through his body and mind.[1] Contemplation of the successful *yogi's* vision of Reality surely helps the emulation of his conduct, which is *Karma-yoga*. Contemplation along these lines helps to eliminate ignorance; and this goes to neutralize the primary mental forces of attraction and repulsion and thus to check the onrush of desires at the source. Thus *Karma-yoga* becomes quite

[1] Cf. *ibid.* V. 8.

practicable for those who can ally it in this way with *Jnāna-yoga*.

This combination may also prove rather stiff for many. A spiritual aspirant (*sādhaka*) may look at the same Divine Unity from a different angle. He may more easily contemplate that he is only an instrument through which God is really doing everything. Seated in the heart of every creature, He is moving everyone like a marionette through His inscrutable power called *Māyā*.[1]

"I am the engine, Thou art the Driver. I am the chariot, Thou art the Charioteer. I am the house, Thou art the Dweller." To think of one's relation with God along these lines is easier than to strive to stand apart as the Witness Self. So long as it is not possible to eliminate the unreal self, it is better to meditate on its relation with God. Through His Divine *Māyā* it has been projected, and through that alone it appears to be doing and experiencing things. By His *Parā Prakriti* (Supreme Cosmic Energy) God appears as myriads of distinct little selves, and by His *Aparā Prakriti* (Lower Cosmic Energy) He appears as the bodies, minds, senses, etc., as well as the material universe. So long as it is not possible for us to meditate on Him as the only Reality and do away with our little 'me' and 'mine', we may very well consider ourselves so many instruments through which God is working out His

[1] Cf. *ibid*. XVIII. 61.

Divine Will. This is why in the *Gita* Sri Krishna said to Arjuna, "I have already killed these people (through My Cosmic Will), you simply behave as the instrument (of My Will)."[1]

"I am the part, Thou art the Whole. I am the wave, Thou art the Ocean. I am the spark, Thou art the Fire." Thus also may the aspirant meditate on his oneness with God and try to eliminate his Primal Ignorance (*anādi Avidyā*).

Easier still is to look upon God as a very near and dear one, related to us very intimately as Father, Mother, Friend, Master, etc., as prescribed by *Bhakti-yoga*. "He has sent me to this world to perform His work. He has entrusted to me the care and well-being of all according to my might. Starting from the family right up to the entire human society, all belong to Him and thrive in His Infinite Love. Their well-being is the concern of my Beloved Father, Mother or Master. I should take my due share in this. Instead of considering myself permanently related to a group of family members, I should look upon them all as His children entrusted to my care. And thus with my community, my nation, my race, and human society. Just as a maid servant takes affectionate care of her master's children, knowing all the while that they do not belong to her but to the master, so should I behave with the members of my family,

[1] *Ibid.* XI. 33.

community, nation, race, and humanity. All property also really belongs to Him. I have to leave them all at death. During life I am only the custodian of His property. I do not own anything. Everything is His. Just as a faithful servant takes due care of his master's property, knowing all the time that it does not belong to him but to the master, so should I deal with all property that appears to be in my possession for the time being." Meditation along these lines is sure to dispel much of our ignorance and conduce to *Karma-yoga*.

Such an outlook developed through this kind of contemplation sanctifies everything about the householder's life. Everything is seen to be linked with God. Selfishness finds no corner to hide itself in. The little self becomes a beloved and faithful agent of God. Everything becomes sacred. Nothing remains to be hated or to be specially attached to. Desires for worldly things are stopped at the source and duties appear as God's own work. They are performed with religious devotion, their fruits being offered to the Lord. Such a devotee bows down to and accepts with equal grace whatever comes, good or evil, believing that it has been decreed by the Beloved Lord for his well-being.

Thus may contemplation on the lines of *Bhakti-yoga* aid the practice of *Karma-yoga*. And this combination suits the majority of earnest souls. Indeed, it is an admirable recipe for those householders who seriously want to reach the goal of liberation (*moksha*).

It is to be noted, however, that for such householders *Karma-yoga* is an essential course of spiritual practice, no matter with what it is combined—*jnāna* or *bhakti*. The combination, of course, depends on the choice of the individual according to his own taste and capacity. In any case, a householder who looks upon Blessedness (*shreyas*) as the supreme object of life, has to strive hard for merging the secular in the spiritual. He has to convert all acts in connection with his various duties into worship. For such complete dedication of oneself through *Karma-yoga* quickly chastens one's mind and speeds up one's spiritual progress.

Thus *Karma-yoga* is surely a wonderful method of transforming worldly life into a life of intense spiritual practice. Usually the final course of spiritual practice (*Nivritti Mārga*) through either *Rāja-yoga*, *Jnāna-yoga* or *Bhakti-yoga* requires a complete detachment from all worldly concerns. For the worldly life with its ties of relationship and burden of duties stands in the way of one-pointed devotion to spiritual practice as prescribed by these *yogas*. This is why the earnest souls usually have to tear themselves away from all earthly relations and renounce all worldly duties. They have to embrace what is called *Sannyāsa*, which is a new life free from all other cares and anxieties than those related to their spiritual practice. This fact naturally gives rise to the popular notion that worldly life is a bar to real spiritual progress. Such life and spirituality come to be looked upon as poles asunder. But *Karma-yoga* dispels this illusion. It shows how worldly life, far from proving a distraction, may speed up one's spiritual advancement. The touch of *yoga* transforms a secular duty into a spiritual endeavour and thus sanctifies worldly life with all its ties of relationship and burden of duties. Seen from the angle of *Karma-yoga*, the social *milieu* is no less congenial to spiritual growth than the seclusion of the forest.

In the *Gitā* it has been pointed out that many like Janaka attained perfection without giving up their worldly duties.[1] The Upanishads also refer to many sages among the kings (*rājarshis*), from whom even the Brāhmins would come to receive *Brahma-vidyā* (Supreme Knowledge). In the Purānas there are numerous instances of people of almost every walk of the householder's life, who attained spiritual eminence through *Karma-yoga*.

Yet *Karma-yoga* is not to be practised by the householders alone. Those *Sannyāsis* (monks) who renounce the world before reaching the stage of equanimity, cannot by-pass this *yoga*. They have to chasten and pacify their minds to a considerable extent through *Karma-yoga*, allied either with *Jnāna*

[1] Cf. *ibid*. III. 20.

or *bhakti*. Else they cannot possibly devote themselves entirely to any other form of intense spiritual practice. And in that case *Sannyāsa* (renunciation of worldly life) has every chance of turning into a life of ease and laziness and runs the risk of ending in a miserable frustration, as pointed out by *Bhagavān* Sri Krishna in the *Gitā*. Indeed, until the mind is purged of attachment and hatred and made fit for one-pointed devotion to any other form of spiritual exercise, *Karma-yoga* is a necessary and essential course for all. Renunciation of worldly life may help one considerably on the spiritual path. But renunciation of all works must naturally follow the elimination of all desires through *Karma-yoga*. So long as the desires are not thus quelled, one's mind can never be hushed into the silence of Divine contemplation (*dhyāna* and *samādhi*).

The *Sannyāsi's* approach, however, to *Karma-yoga* is fundamentally different from the householder's. The householder's duties arise out of his loyalty to social relations. The *Sannyāsi's* duties on the other hand, are concerned with the service of humanity without preference for any group on the score of earthly relations. No family, caste, creed or colour is to stand between him and humanity. The material and spiritual well-being of all offers him an unlimited scope for the practice of *Karma-yoga* till his mind is cleared of all impurities.

Second Part

XIV

THE PROPHETS AND SCRIPTURES

MUCH ground has been covered. Some of the main contents of Hinduism have been dealt with. The idea of *samsāra* (rebirth) and *mukti* (release) followd by preliminary (*Pravritti Mārga*) and final (*Nivritti Mārga*) courses of spiritual practice has been gone through. And, in connection with the last, we have been acquainted with the four basic types of spiritual practice (*sādhanā*), namely, *Rāja-yoga*, *Jnāna-yoga*, *Bhakti-yoga* and *Karma-yoga*. Of course, so far all these have been put in a nutshell.

However, we are now in a position to view Hinduism as a whole. For this let us scan and add up its essential features that mark it out from all other religions.

Every religion has at its origin at least one Prophet and one book of revelations known as the Scriptures. And the teachings of each religion contain a central core of spiritual truths embedded in an outer growth of rituals and mythology. Thus the Prophet, the Scriptures, spiritual truths, rituals and mythology are the five important constituents of a religion. A general idea, therefore, of these five essential elements of Hinduism will give a whole view of this religion.

PROPHET

Hinduism has no Prophet at its source. Spiritual truths were first discovered and announced by the Vedic seers (*rishis*), many of whom have not cared to leave their names behind. And even those whose names are found on record are not looked upon as Prophets. The collections of spiritual truths (the Vedas) are honoured more than their discoverers.

Yet the Hindus believe that God incarnates Himself again and again in flesh and blood whenever religion (*dharma*) gets perverted and irreligion (*adharma*) gains prominence. They hold that on such occasions God comes down to this earth with a physical body to show the right path of deliverance to the righteous ones and to inflict due punishment on the wicked ones for their necessary correction.[1]

Surely, the Vedic Religion teaches that God is in every creature, in fact, in everything. But there hangs, by His inscrutable power called *Māyā*, a veil of ignorance covering Self-knowledge. The *jivas* (living beings) have to remove this veil, bit by bit, by their own efforts. In fact, this is the secret urge of evolution in the subhuman world. On the human plane these efforts become conscious ones. Man has to uncover the Divinity That lies concealed within him. This is precisely his *dharma*. Yet, from time to time, man misses this central truth about

[1] Cf. *Gita* IV. 7–8.

his life and its spiritual aim. In his confusion he goes so far as to laugh away his potential divinity as an absurd idea. He cannot make himself believe that he can ever rise above the instincts of lust and greed, hatred and strife, conceit and crass selfishness. Manifestation of Divinity looks like an empty dream. Bereft of this inner spirit, religion with its rituals and dogmas becomes a mockery. At this stage people do not mind using religion even as a cover for dirty and nefarious deeds. When in this way the ascent of man towards Divinity is seriously endangered, God descends on earth to release the clogged wheels of the spiritual progress of mankind. Through His life man sees vividly the ideal to be reached by him. What manifestation of Divinity in man looks like becomes clear. His teachings dispel the gathering doubts, and His life furnishes humanity with a fresh, living and luminous model which they are to copy for their upward growth. This gives a new impetus to the ascent of man towards godhood. Religion thus gets a fresh lease of life. Humanity starts over again towards its spiritual goal of Divinity.

This is how the Hindus regard the purpose of an Incarnation of God. They rightly call Him an *Avatāra*, that is, a descent of the Universal Spirit (*ava*—below, and the Sanskrit root *tri*—to cross). God, as it were, crosses the border dividing His Divine Essence from His physical manifestation, that is, the material universe. Unlike the *jivas*, no veil of ignorance hangs before the *Avatāra*. With *Māyā* under His complete control and with the full blaze of Self-knowledge, the Lord of the universe appears to be born and to live for working out His Divine purpose. The *Avatāra* is a manifestation of Divinity from above, which man has to manifest from below.

The Purānas refer to innumerable *Avatāras*.[1] Some are reported in the *Chandi* to have appeared in the *Devaloka*. However, ten *Avatāras* on earth are prominently mentioned in the Purānas, namely, *Matsya* (fish), *Kurma* (tortoise), *Varāha* (boar), *Nri-simha* (man-lion), *Vāmana* (dwarf), *Parashurāma*, *Rāmachandra*, *Balarāma*, Buddha and *Kalki*. The fact that this list omits the name of *Bhagavān* Sri Krishna shows that it is not at all exhaustive. Through many more forms He may very well be expected to come in future. Neither time nor space can limit the descent of God as *Avatāra*. Whenever there has been an urgent need for restoring the spiritual balance of the human society or any of its major portions, the *Avatāra* has come. And the same will happen over and over again throughout the entire future. The Hindus believe in the operation of such a spiritual law of Divine Incarnation. This is why it is not unlikely for the Hindus to regard Buddha and even Christ and Muhammed

[1] *Vide Shrimad Bhāgavatam*, also *Chandi* in *Mārkandeya Purāna*.

as *Avatāras*. Within the historical period many outstanding spiritual personalities have appeared in India and come to be regarded by the Hindus as Incarnations of God. Buddha, Shankara and Chaitanya are prominent among them. In our days, Sri Rāmakrishna (1836–86) has come to be looked upon by many as an *Avatāra*.

A word about the popular list of ten *Avatāras* is deemed necessary. The mention of fish, tortoise, boar, man-lion and dwarf in the list may trouble many of us. Many rationalists read in this a suggestion regarding the order of biological evolution. We need not bother about evolution and all that in this connection. Nor have we any reason to feel small for the presence of these subhuman specimens on the list of *Avatāras*. The Hindu conception of God is wide enough to accommodate all these. It is possible for God, who has manifested Himself as the entire universe with its contents, to appear in any guise for the fulfilment of His Divine purpose. And the time of these *Avatāras* is mentioned to be in the hoary, legendary past. We practically know nothing about that period. So we need hardly waste our energy for either verifying or explaining away the statement of the Purānas. We know that it is possible for Him to appear in these forms and that is enough for us. His life and work are distinct from the commonplace. The manifestations may look like that, yet they are entirely of another order.

They are Divine.[1] And one who grasps this truth gets released from *samsāra*.

Sometimes God incarnates Himself in a female body and appears as a consort of an *Avatāra* in a male body. Sitā, the holy consort of Sri Rāmachandra, and Vishnupriyā, that of Sri Chaitanya, are regarded by the Hindus as such Divine Incarnations. So also is the holy consort of Sri Rāmakrishna, popularly known as the Holy Mother, looked upon by numerous devotees.

The Hindus, moreover, believe that besides the Incarnations of God, prominent spiritual personalities of another order appear on earth from time to time. They come as *Āchāryas* (Teachers) to explain the correct import of the *Shāstras* and to give a spiritual lift to humanity. They are perfected souls living normally anywhere in the higher worlds. Sometimes they accompany an *Avatara* as His companions (*Pārshadas*) to serve as the blessed instruments of His Divine mission. Sometimes they come singly as divine messengers to spread the eternal truths about Divinity and the spiritual end and aim of human life. Often they are regarded as manifestations of one or other of the infinite powers (*vibhutis*) of God. However, their supernormal spiritual lives and teachings give them also the look of Prophets. Such is the spiritual power (*aishwarya*) displayed by the personalities of this order that it

[1] Cf. *Gita* IV. 9.

is difficult to distinguish between them and an *Avatāra*. It baffles human understanding to say definitely whether Sri Shankara and Sri Rāmānuja were Incarnations of God or personalities of this order. However, Swāmi Vivekānanda of our days is regarded by many as one of the latest representatives of this order.

Thus it is clear that though Hinduism does not claim to have any Prophet at its source, it holds elaborate and definite views regarding the advent and mission of Prophets.

SCRIPTURES

The second essential element of a religion on our list is the Scriptures. This has already been dealt with in a separate chapter.[1] Yet the striking features of the Hindu Scriptures are worth mentioning over again in the present connection.

The Hindu word for the Scriptures is *Shāstra*. This very word gives a clue to the Hindu point of view regarding their Scriptures. The word is derived from the Sanskrit root *shās* (meaning to rule, to govern). And it literally means that by which one is governed. The Hindu *Shāstras* are not regarded as a body of revelations that require only our assent, or that prescribe only what we have to do within the temple. The *Shāstras* are to govern our entire life so that we may advance spiritually towards perfection.

[1] Chap. III.

The foremost of the Hindu *Shāstras* are the
Vedas. Here again, the Hindus do not look upon
the Vedas as only books of revelation. By the word
'Vedas' they refer to the entire body of spiritual
truths that exist eternally. These are absolutely
impersonal. The seers (*rishis*) discovered some of
these, which are found recorded in the books
popularly known as the Vedas. Wherever and whenever spiritual truths have been discovered, a portion
of the Vedas has been disclosed, for the Vedas stand
for the entire body of spiritual truths. They cannot
therefore, in their original sense, belong to any clan
or community. They belong to the entire human
society. Moreover, they do not belong to any particular time. They are eternal. Some portions of them
have been discovered. Some more may yet be done
in future. Who knows?

The third point to be noted regarding the Hindu
Shāstras is their variety, such as *Shruti*, *Smriti*,
Darshana, *Itihāsa*, *Purāna*, *Tantra*, etc. To bring the
subtle spiritual truths within everybody's range of
understanding, they have been presented in various
ways in the different *Shāstras*. Moreover, different
approaches to the same goal have been emphasized
by some of these *Shāstras*.

A word about the *Smritis* may be mentioned. The
Smritis, laying down codes of individual conduct and
social regulations, are not given eternal values.
They vary from time to time according to the

changed conditions of the society. Whenever any such exigency arises, outstanding spiritual personalities appear to give such revised versions of the *Smriti*. Though variable, they must always conform to the fundamental truths revealed in the *Shruti* (Vedas).

These few points in connection with the Hindu *Shāstras* are enough for the present purpose.

XV
ISHWARA
GOD

THE third essential factor on our list is 'spiritual truths'. This comprises all that has been realized by the Hindu seers and revealed through the *Shāstras* about God, nature and soul. Some of these we have come across casually in the course of the previous topics. We now propose to elaborate these to some extent.

Though the Hindu pantheon teems with millions of deities, God, according to the Hindus, is one and only one. In fact He is the sole Reality. What He is really like, nobody can say or think of. That is beyond the range of our mind and speech. From where mind and speech recoil, baffled in their quest.[1]

He is certainly not like anything we know of. The things in nature exist in space and time, and are subject to ceaseless change under the law of causation. They have birth, growth and decay. They are made of parts and are, therefore, liable to dissolution. But *Brahman*, the Supreme Spirit, is one undivided whole and is beyond time, space and causation. He is Changeless, Eternal, Infinite, ever Free and beyond the reach of our senses. He cannot

[1] *Tait. Up.* II. 9.

be limited by any form or attribute.[1] He is Transcendental. 'Neti neti' (not this, not this)[2] is all that may be said about Him.

This is what the Shāstras call Parabrahman, which, though not like anything we know of, is however, not a mere void (shunya), nor an insentient something. It is the very essence of Existence, Consciousness and Bliss. So do the Hindu Shāstras refer to the Transcendent One. This universe was but Existence at the beginning, one only without a second.[3] Brahman is Truth, Consciousness and Infinity.[4] Brahman is Consciousness and Bliss.[5] The light of the sun, moon, stars, lightning or the fire does not reach Him; He shining, all these luminaries shine; by His light the universe is illumined.[6] It is by His light of Consciousness that we become aware of everything. He is said to be the ear of our ears, the mind of our minds, and so on.[7] In fact, He is the innermost Being in us. It is by the touch of His Consciousness that the myriads of little groups of body, mind and senses behave as jivas (creatures), as subjects of action and experience.[8]

Yet all these references of the Shāstras do not and cannot describe Parabrahman as He really is. These are at best suggestive hints of the great Transcendent Reality. Just as the expression 'What roaring

[1] Cf. Bri. Up. III. 8. 8.
[3] Chh. Up. VI. 2. 1.
[5] Bri. Up. III. 9. 28.
[7] Cf. Ke. Up. I. 1. 2.
[2] Cf. ibid. III. 9. 26.
[4] Tait. Up. II. 1. 3.
[6] Cf. Ka. Up. II. 2. 15.
[8] Cf. Ka. Up. I. 3. 4.

waves!' cannot make one who has not seen the sea
visualize it, so also all these expressions of the
Shāstras cannot make one comprehend what *Parabrahman* is like. All that we may gather from these
is that *Nirguna Brahman* is not a void, nor an
insentient something, but that He is the source and
support of every object and experience in nature,
that He is One without a second. There is neither
I nor thou, neither subject nor object. *Parabrahman*
is Impersonal God, whom the *Shāstras* refer to by
the pronoun 'That', and not by 'He' or 'She'.

The Hindu *Shāstras* hold that such a Reality is
at the source of creation. The universe comes out
of *Brahman*, rests in Him and merges in Him,[1] and
this goes on eternally in a cycle. Just as the spider
throws out the web from within itself and draws it
in, so also does God with the universe. Just as trees
and plants shoot up from the earth, just as hair
grows out of one's body, so does the universe come
out of God.[2] He pervades the whole of nature;
everything within nature has its existence in and
through *Brahman*.[3] God has not created the world
out of nothing. He has projected it out of Himself.
He is both the efficient and material cause of the
universe.

But the universe (*Brahmānda*) does not cover
His entire being. It is no doubt in Him, yet He is

[1] Cf. *Tait. Up.* III. 6.   [2] Cf. *Mund. Up.* I. 1. 7.
[3] Cf. *Ish. Up.* I. also cf. *Bri. Up.* III. 8. 4, 11.

eternally aloof and apart from it. This is suggested by the *Shāstras* when they say that the universe rests on a portion of His being.[1]

Thus our *Shāstras* refer to God both as the Transcendent and the Immanent One. He is Formless and Changeless, yet He is the basis of the ever-changing infinite forms of nature. And it is under the mighty rule of the Immanent One that everything in nature is kept in its proper place, every function is regulated, order and harmony everywhere are maintained.[2] The Transcendent One whom the senses, mind and intellect can never know, resides within everything and controls it from within. He is the *Antaryāmi*. And He is verily our Self (*Ātman*).[3]

When the universe drops from one's consciousness, as in *nirvikalpa samādhi*, He is realized as *Nirguna Nirākāra Brahman*. But as long as we are conscious of the universe, the same *Brahman* appears as its Projector, Protector and Ruler, and we call Him *Shakti* and *Ishwara*. *Brahman* and *Shakti* are inseparable. They are different phases of the same Being. Just as the power of burning cannot be separated from fire, *Shakti*, that is, the Power of Becoming, cannot be separated from *Brahman*. Just as there is no substantial difference between the snake at rest and the snake in motion, so there

---

[1] Cf. *Rg. Vd.* X. 90. 3, also cf. *Gitā* X. 42 & *Bri. Up.* III. 9. 26.
[2] Cf. *Bri. Up.* III. 8. 9.   [3] Cf. *ibid.* III. 7.

is none between *Brahman* and *Shakti*. Just as a
mere change of pose does not affect the identity of
a person, so the pose of *Ishwara* does not affect the
identity of *Brahman*.

The *Saguna* aspect of *Brahman* is what we call
Shakti or *Ishwara*. *Ishwara*, the Lord of Creation, is
Personal God. He is the All-pervading Supreme
Master of the universe. *Nirguna Brahman* is referred
to in the *Shāstras* as the highest state of the Personal
God. ('*Tad Vishnoh paramam padam*'). Sri Krishna
says in the *Gitā*, "That is My highest abode."[1]

However, it is to the Personal God, *Ishwara*, that
most of the religions point. He is the Formless One,
who by His Omnipotent Will manifests Himself as
the universe with all its contents. This is His play
(*lilā*). He is the father, the mother, the ordainer, the
creator; He is the path, the goal, the upholder, the
master, the witness, the abode, the refuge and the
supreme well-wisher; He is the source, end and
resting place of all; He is the indestructible seed of
the universe.[2] He transcends all that is mutable as
also the immutable, and covering all sustains all as
Changeless *Ishwara*, the Supreme Being (*Purushottama*).[3] Whoever worships God, worships Him and
Him alone.

According to the Hindu *Shāstras*, the Formless
Lord, however, assumes various forms by His

---

[1] *Gita* XV. 6.   [2] Cf. *ibid.* IX. 17–18.   [3] Cf. *ibid.* XV. 17–18.

Māyā.[1] In fact, all names and all forms are His. Besides, He has many divine forms, in any of which He may be seen by the pure souls. These forms are just like different suits of garments, under which God is always the same. He puts on these forms only to make Himself accessible to us. So also He appears in different forms as *Avatāra*.

Thus according to the *Hindu Shāstras*, though God is one and one only, He appears as many. Though He is absolutely Formless (*Nirākāra*), He appears through myriads of forms. Though He is not limited by an attribute (*Nirguna*), He is verily the source and support of all attributes. He is Impersonal as well as Personal. Even as Personal God with attributes (*Saguna*), He is worshipped as the Formless One (*Nirākāra*) as well as through innumerable names and forms (*Sākāra*). This is why it is quite natural for the Hindus to regard even *Āllāh* and God as just two alternative names of the selfsame Lord of the universe, whom they call *Ishwara*.

Yet among the Hindus there is a diversity of choice of one or other aspect of God. Different sects (*sampradāya*) hold to different set views. Some hold that God is without form (*Nirākāra*) and without attributes (*Nirguna*); some believe that He is Formless, Yet He has attributes; some others hold that He has eternal forms and attributes. The last group, again, is subdivided according to the choice of

[1] Cf. *Ṛg. Vd.* VI. 47. 18, also cf. *Bri. Up.* II. 5. 19.

different forms. Thus some of them are Shaivas, some Vaishnavas, some Shāktas and so on.

God and His glories (*mahimā*) being infinite, approaches to Him may be innumerable. So this division and subdivision of the Hindu society into various sects according to the choice of one or other aspect of God is quite natural. It only shows the richness of Hinduism that throws open so many approaches to Divinity suited to different tastes, temperaments and capacities. No sect, however, should claim its own view-point to be the only correct one. This gives rise to sectarian squabbles and undermines the strength and solidarity of the Hindu community. It generates hatred and jealousy, which are the very reverse of spirituality.

The Vedic seers realized the great truth that what God really is, can never be delineated by mind or speech. He is not exhausted by all that the different sects or even religions say about Him. He is all these and more. Each sect or religion holds to a reading of the same Reality from a particular angle, as it were. Each view is correct so far as it goes, but it certainly cannot convey the whole truth about Him who is beyond mind and speech. The *Rig-Veda* declares, "One alone exists, sages call It by various names."[1]

Sri Rāmakrishna used to make this point clear through the following interesting parables:

[1] *Rg. Vd.* I. 164. 46.

'Four blind men went out to know an elephant. One touched the leg of the elephant and said, "The elephant is like a pillar." The second touched the trunk and said, "The elephant is like a thick club." The third touched the belly and said, "The elephant is like a big jar." The fourth touched the ears and said "The elephant is like a big winnowing basket." Thus they began to dispute about it amongst themselves. A passer-by, seeing them thus quarrelling said, "What is it you are disputing about?" Then they stated the question and asked him to arbitrate. The man said, "None of you has seen the elephant. The elephant is not like a pillar, its legs are like pillars. It is not like a winnowing basket, its ears are like winnowing baskets. It is not like a stout club, its proboscis is like a club. The elephant is the combination of all these, of its legs, ears, belly and trunk." It is in this way that all those who have seen only one aspect of the Deity quarrel among themselves.'[1]

'Two persons were hotly disputing as to the colour of a chameleon. One said, "The chameleon on that palm tree is of a beautiful red colour." The other contradicted him saying, "You are mistaken, the chameleon is not red, but blue." Being unable to settle the matter by argument, both went to a person who always lived under that tree and had watched the chameleon in all its phases of colour.

[1] *Sayings of Sri Rāmakrishna*, p. 287.

One of the disputants said, "Sir, is not the chameleon on that tree of a red colour?" That person replied, "Yes, sir." The other disputant said, "What
do you say? How is that? Surely it is not red but
blue." That person again humbly replied, "Yes,
sir." The person knew that the chameleon constantly changes its colour: thus he said "Yes" to
both the conflicting statements. The *Satchidānanda*
likewise has various forms. The devotee who has
seen God in one aspect only knows that aspect alone.
But he alone who has seen Him in manifold aspects
can say, "All these forms are of one God, for God
is multiform." He is formless and with form and
many are His forms which no one knows."[1]

By these analogies Sri Rāmakrishna pointed out
that the different views of the different sects are correct but partial representations of God.

This also explains why the Hindus worship millions of gods. Many of these are different representations of the same *Ishwara*. Many others represent
one or other of His infinite powers (*vibhuti*).
By worshipping any of these the same Lord is
worshipped.

The rest are deities (*devatā*). They are created
beings holding exalted positions. They have been
promoted to that stage by their meritorious deeds
on earth. The greatest of them is the first created
being, called *Hiranyagarbha*. He is Cosmic Intel-

[1] *Ibid.* p. 207.

ligence. He has infinite powers, for he comprises all that is manifested. *Agni*, *Āditya* and such other deities represent one or other of his powers. As these powers are infinite, the deities are also infinite. But they are all comprehended in the one *deva*, namely, *Hiranyagarbha*.[1] By worshipping any of the deities, he is worshipped; and by worshipping him, all of them are worshipped. And this *Hiranyagarbha*, through a cosmic being, is a glorified *jiva*. These deities, therefore, should never be confused with *Ishwara*, who is Eternal and the Master of all. Of course, they may serve as symbols (*pratikas*) of God, just as man may be worshipped as His symbol.[2]

Thus amidst the innumerable diversities of forms of *Ishwara* as well as of the *devas*, Hinduism imparts a vision of fundamental unity.

[1] Cf. *Bri. Up.* III. 9. 9.   [2] See *supra.* Chap. XI

XVI

BRAHMĀNDA

NATURE

SUBTLE

Hinduism holds that the universe (*Brahmānda*) has no beginning in time. It has been appearing and disappearing alternately, in a perfect rhythm, as it were. It comes into being, lasts for a period and then melts away. These steps are known as *Srishti*, *Sthiti* and *Pralaya*. These three make one complete cycle, which has been repeating itself eternally.

Something akin to it is experienced by us all almost everyday. *Brahmānda* appears and disappears alternately as we pass through the states of waking and sleep. To the individual mind in deep sleep it ceases to exist. This also is *pralaya*. Only it is limited by the consciousness of the sleeping individuals. This temporary dissolution during sleep is called *nitya pralaya* (dissolution of everyday experience).

Now, what would happen if all individuals within creation would fall asleep at one time? No one, in that case, would surely be aware of the universe. It would be blotted out altogether. Hinduism holds that such a thing actually takes place. The sum total of all minds is the cosmic mind, which is possessed by a deity. This deity is the first-born individual, with almost infinite powers. He is referred to in the Upanishads by various names, such as *Hiranyagarbha*, *Sutrātmā*, *Aparabrahman*, *Mahadbrahman*, *Prāna*. He is sometimes sublimated into a form of *Ishwara* and called *Brahmā* by the Purānas. When *Brahmā*, comprising all minds, falls asleep there is *naimittika Pralaya*, that is, occasional Dissolution. When he wakes up, *Brahmānda* becomes manifest, and this is *Srishti*. The *Srishti* and *Sthiti* period corresponds to *Brahmā's* day and the *Pralaya* period to his night.[1]

What really takes place when we go to sleep? If we can find that out, it will give us a clue to what happens during *Pralaya*. During sound sleep we are not aware of any existence with name and form. Not a trace of the external world nor of the details of our own individuality is left. No action, no experience, no thought, no desire is there. It is almost a perfect blank. We forget everything, even our names and appearances, our homes and occupations. But as soon as we wake up, all these come back to our consciousness. Where had they been so long? Obviously they were not totally destroyed during sleep. Hinduism holds that all thoughts, all desires, were certainly there in the mind in a potential state as subtle impressions (*samskāras*); otherwise they could not reappear on waking up. During sleep somehow they are reduced to an

[1] Cf. *Gita* VIII. 17–19.

unmanifested (*avyakta*) condition, which becomes manifest again after the sleep is over.

The features of a big tree lie potentially within a tiny seed in the form of some unseen energy. It is this energy that manifests itself in due course as the tree. It is verily the cause that brings the tree into being. The tree may very well be said to be residing within the seed in an unmanifested causal (*kārana*) state. Just so, during sound sleep all that compose our individuality—our thoughts, desires, inclinations, judgment, memory and all that—reside within us in a causal state in the form of some unseen energy. As a matter of fact our intellect (*buddhi*), mind and the senses are then reduced to causal state, that is why they cease functioning and we lose all our bearings during sound sleep. This unmanifested causal state is said to be our causal body (*kārana sharira*), where during deep sleep our consciousness rests after retiring from the physical and mental bodies.

This is how the sleep phenomenon is explained by our *Shāstras*. The same thing takes place when the Cosmic Intelligence (*Hiranyagarbha*) falls alseep. As his consciousness retires to his *kārana sharira*, all minds within creation, being portions of the cosmic mind, together with all objects of their experience go back to the causal state. Everything in nature, gross and fine, is reduced to the unmanifested causal state composing *Hiranyagarbha's kārana sharira*.

Thus when the cosmic mind of *Hiranyagarbha* goes to sleep, there is cosmic Dissolution; and this is known as *naimittika Pralaya*; *Srishti* begins with its waking up. And these follow each other alternately.[1]

A similar Dissolution takes place at the end of a cycle, that is, *Hiranyagarbha's* span of life,[2] when he becomes disembodied altogether and merges into *Parabrahman*. Everything in nature then goes back to the unmanifested infinite energy (*Shakti*) known as *Avyakta* or *Prakriti*. The cosmic Dissolution brought about in this way by *Hiranyagarbha's* liberation is called *prākrita Pralaya*. At the outset of the next cycle another being appears as *Hiranyagarbha* due to the outstanding merits acquired by him during the previous cycle.[3]

However, *Hiranyagarbha*, the first-born *jiva* of a cycle, is endowed with infinite powers of knowledge, will and action. The rest of Creation is his doing. This is why *Brahmā* is introduced by the Purānas as the Creator.

How does *Brahmā* create? He does not create anything out of a void. He projects the *Brahmānda* out of himself. He becomes the universe. Whatever

---

[1] *Hiranyagarbha's* day (period of his waking and sleeping or periodic creation and dissolution) is called a *kalpa*.

[2] Consists of one hundred years of his measure, his day being equal to 4,320,000,000 human years.

[3] There is yet another kind of *Pralaya*. On the attainment of full knowledge of *Parabrahman*, the *Brahmānda* together with its root cause *Avidyā* or Primal Nescience disappears completely. This is why it is called *ātyantika Pralaya*, that is, absolute Dissolution. In every other kind of *Pralaya*, the unmanifested causal state (*avyakta* or *kārana*) remains.

he wills, he becomes. And he wills according to a set pattern, which he discovers by meditating on exactly what happened during the previous cycle. By meditation he finds all that have been lying in the causal state and waiting to be manifested. According to the order of the previous cycle and the urgency of manifestation he proceeds to project out of himself myriads of objects, gross and fine, by his mere will.

We may have a faint idea of how all this takes place at the mere will of the cosmic mind if we compare with it our own experiences during the dream-state. Who weaves our dreams? Obviously our minds. Out of what material? Obviously out of their own stuff. Whatever our minds desire, they see out there in the dream. Rather, the minds themselves become all that they desire. In light sleep, when the mind gets away from the grip of the external world, it displays this wonderful power of transforming itself into anything and everything at its sweet will. Really, it beats a magician!

If that is possible for the individual mind, the cosmic mind may very well weave out of itself the universe at its will. *Brahmā* does it deliberately and according to a plan; while we weave our dreams in the subconscious state. This, of course, is a great difference. Yet, the two phenomena are very much alike. What *Brahmā* discovers by meditation he wills, and what he wills he sees. What he sees, our minds, being portions of the cosmic mind, perceive within the limits of their capacity.

Now, how does *Brahmā* himself come into being? Who creates him? Moreover, being a *jiva*, he must be an embodied soul as every one of us is. Now, what may be his body and what his spirit?

These queries take us into deeper water. The last two may be disposed of first. The cosmic mind is his body and God Himself is the spirit within.

The sum total of all subtle bodies (*sukshma* or *linga sharira*) is his body. It consists of three concentric chambers or sheaths (*kosha*), known as the *vijnānamaya, manomaya* and *prānamaya kosha*. The *vijnānamaya kosha* consists of the intellect (*buddhi*) and the five subtle senses of knowledge (*jnānendriya*); endowed with the power of knowledge, this chamber (*kosha*) is the seat of the subject of experience and action. The *manomaya kosha* consists of the mind and the five subtle senses of knowledge and is endowed with the power of will. The *prānamaya kosha* consists of the five *prānas*[1] and the five subtle senses of action (*karmendriya*), and it is endowed with the power of action.

All these sheaths (*kosha*) constituting *Hiranya-garbha's* body are made of five elementary (*sukshma*) *bhutas*, which are exceedingly fine and are also known as *tanmātras*. The word '*bhuta*' literally means

---

[1] *Prāna* (vital energy) is said to be of five kinds corresponding to different physiological functions. The five *Prānas* are called *prāna, apāna, samāna, udāna* and *vyāna*.

what has come into being, an entity as opposed to the unmanifested (*avyakta*). *Tanmātra* means 'that alone'; hence it stands for an elementary *bhuta* so long as it is not mixed up with others.[1]

The five elementary *bhutas* are said to the *ākāsha*, *vāyu*, *tejas*, *ap* and *kshiti*. These should not be confused with what we mean by ether, air, fire, water and earth. The *tanmātras* are far more subtle than these and belong to a different order. The analytical approach of the Hindu *rishis* is altogether different from that of modern science.[2]

These *tanmātras*, however, do not emerge all at once out of *Avyakta*. *Ākāsha* comes out first, a portion of it transforms itself into *vāyu*, a portion of which again transforms itself into *tejas*; from *tejas* in this way comes out *ap* and from *ap kshiti*.

One thing more has to be noted in this connection. *Avyakta*, out of which the *tanmātras* emerge, is said to be characterized by three traits depending on its three distinct components, namely, *sattwa*, *rajas* and *tamas*. *Sattwa* is that principle in nature which goes to illumine things, that is, to reveal them to our consciousness. *Rajas* is that which brings about all changes; it is the dynamic element in nature. *Tamas* is the element of ignorance and inertia. The stamp of these three constituents is found on all that come out of *Avyakta*. Even the elementary *bhutas* or *tanmātras* bear this stamp. Each

---

[1] See *infra* Chap. XVII.   [2] See *infra* Chap. XVII.

is said to have an illumining (*sāttwika*), a dynamic (*rājasika*) and an inert (*tāmasika*) part.

The illumining portions of each of the five elementary *bhutas*—*ākāsha, vāyu, tejas, ap* and *kshiti*—build up respectively the subtle senses of knowledge corresponding to the ears, skin, eyes, tongue and nose (*shrotra, twak, chakshu, jihvā* and *nāsikā*). The illumining portions of them all combine to compose the intellect (*buddhi*) and mind. Similarly the dynamic portions of the *bhutas* separately form the five subtle senses of action and jointly form the five *prānas*. The three chambers (*kosha*) composing *Brahmā's* body are built up in this way by the illumining and dynamic portions of the *tanmātras*. *Brahmā* has such a cosmic subtle body (*sukshma sharira*). In it is comprehended the fine bodies (*sukshma sharira*) of all living beings.

XVII

BRAHMĀNDA (*continued*)

GROSS

The inert (*tāmasika*) portions of the *tanmātras* get compounded with one another by a particular process known as *panchikarana* and form what are known as the gross *bhutas*.[1] Each gross *bhuta* is made up of all the five kinds of *tanmātras* or subtle *bhutas* in a particular proportion. Gross *ākāsha*, for instance, has in its composition half of subtle *ākāsha* and one-eighth of each of the remaining four subtle *bhutas*, gross *vāyu* has half of subtle *vāyu* and one-eighth of each of the rest; and so on.

These gross *bhutas* compose the physical bodies of the *jivas*, their habitations in the shape of various worlds (*loka*) as well as all the articles of their use. These entities composed by the gross *bhutas* range from the very coarse and dull to the very fine and bright. However, all this takes place by *Hiranyagarbha's* will. He appears to condense himself, so to speak, as the visible universe. By this process is born another cosmic being called *Virāt* who has the entire physical universe as his body and God as his soul.

Hinduism holds, as we have seen, that *Srishti* has no beginning in time. Each Creation (*Srishti*) is

[1] Cf. *Ved. Par.* Chap. VII.

preceded by Dissolution (*Pralaya*) and each Dissolution by Creation, and this has been going on
eternally. Why does it so happen? The Hindu
Shāstras declare that there is a causal link between
Dissolution and Creation. The inexorable law of
karma forges this link. This law, according to
Hinduism, is the supreme law of causation that
determines each Creation and everything within
it. The actions, experiences and desires of the *jivas*
of the previous cycle (*kalpa*) lie in the causal state
during the state of Dissolution. And it is for the
fruition of these that during Creation all *jivas*,
beginning with *Hiranyagarbha*, come into being
together with their various habitations (*loka*) and
materials for their use like food, drink etc. They
are to experience pain and pleasure according to
their bad and good deeds (*karma*) performed during
the previous cycle. It is for this that they come and
are surrounded by myriads of objects of experience.
Thus in *Pralaya* (Dissolution) lies the seed out of
which the *Brahmānda* shoots up like a tree. As a tree
is preceded by a seed, and again the seed by a tree,
so also is *Srishti* preceded by *Pralaya* and *Pralaya* by
Srishti.

The *jivas* hold the centre of the stage. They are
to reap the fruits of their action through experience
(*bhoga*), and that is why the entire universe comes
into existence. Hence the latter is resolved into two
constituent groups, namely, the subjects (*bhoktā*)

and objects (*bhogya*) of experience. The *jivas* belong to the former group and all other things to the latter. From this view-point the *Brahmānda* or *Jagat* is characterized by these two groups of entities,[1] the sentient and the insentient.

The *jivas* experience the world through the senses of knowledge, which are so many instruments of perception (*bhoga*). Each of these conveys to them a particular aspect of the world of experience, and this is said to be its *vishaya* (object of perception). The five senses of knowledge,[2] namely, ears, skin, eyes, tongue and nose have sound, touch, colour, taste and smell as their respective *vishayas*.[3] These five classes of sense-perception are all that the *jivas* are concerned with in the external world. These practically compose their entire external world of experience (*bhogya*).

Now, the sense-perceptions are produced only when the senses are stirred up by stimuli from the external world. Light waves, for instance, stimulate the eyes (*chakshu*) to produce the sense-perception of colour (*rupa*). The external world, therefore, according to this view, consists only of such sense-stimuli.

Gross *ākāsha* stirs up the perception of sound only; *vāyu* stirs up the perception of sound and touch, *tejas* of those of sound, touch and colour

---

[1] '*Bhoktri-bhogya lakshana.*'
[2] *Shrotra, twak, chakshu, jihvā* and *nāsikā*
[3] *Shabda, sparsha, rupa, rasa* and *gandha.*

(*rupa*), *ap* of all these plus taste (*rasa*) and *kshiti* of all the five *vishayas* including smell. It is to be noticed that each succeeding one in the series stirs up the sensation of one more *vishaya* than the preceding *bhuta*; this additional one is said to be its special property (*guna*). Thus sound is the special property of *ākāsha*, touch of *vāyu*, colour of *tejas*, taste of *ap* and smell of *kshiti*.

These gross *bhutas* are thus looked upon as different groups of sense-stimuli. They are of the nature of energy and not of matter. Though their names suggest physical entities like ether, air, fire, water and earth, they are nothing but modes of *Prakriti*, the infinite Cosmic Energy. What we call physical entities are to the Hindus nothing but the Absolute (*Parabrahman*) seen through different modes of the Cosmic Energy (*Prakriti*).[1] From this view-point physical existence is absolutely non-material. The look of matter is deceptive.

Thus before the analytical vision of the Hindu seers the entire universe came to be resolved into subjects of experience (*bhoktā*) and objects of experience (*bhogya*), the experience of external objects again into five classes of sense-perception (*vishaya*), and the external world into five groups of sense-stimuli known as the gross (*sthula*) *bhutas*. The analysis, therefore, is purely psychological and not physical. So even the gross *bhutas* should not be

[1] See *infra* Chap. XVIII.

11

confused with the elements of modern science which have been supposed so long to be the material units of the physical world. The *bhutas* belong to an entirely different order. They are highly subtle sense-stimuli and that is about all that they stand for.

Even if the *bhutas* are assumed to be nothing more than physical entities like ether, air, etc., the following interpretation in support of such classification of the physical world may be considered.

Each of the names may be suggestive and stand for a group of allied objects. Earth (*kshiti*), for instance, may stand for all solids, water (*ap*) for all liquids and air (*vāyu*) for all gases. These three, therefore, cover all matter found in the three different states, namely solid, liquid and gas. Fire (*agni*) may stand for the phenomena[1] of heat and visible light, and ether (*ākāsha*) for the all-pervasive subtle medium through which light waves etc. pass. Do not these five groups of entities cover the entire range of physical existence perceived by us through the five senses? Indeed, the division is complete.

The scientist's division of the world into elements and their atoms, on the other hand, has already become meaningless. The atoms are no longer held

---

[1] *Agni* (fire) stands for the phenomena of heat and visible light as objects of perception and not for heat and light energy. All forms of physical, chemical and biological energy are viewed by the Hindus as modifications of *prāna*, which again is a manifestation of *Prakriti*, the infinite Cosmic Energy.

as ultimate constituents of matter. They have been resolved into energy units (electrons, protons, etc.). The analytical approach of the physicist has penetrated the deceptive outlook of matter. Matter has become dematerialized. It may be noted that this finding of modern science has gone a step ahead towards confirming the Hindu view of nature.

We have seen that the different *bhutas* stimulate different groups of sense-perceptions. So far as air, fire, water and earth are concerned, the group of sense-perceptions related to each of them is quite in order. But how may ether give rise to the sensation of sound? The scientist's ether is beyond the reach of any of our senses. It is almost an imaginary substance through which waves of radiant energy travel. According to them, sound is produced only by the vibration of solids, liquids and gases, and sound stimuli must travel through such material medium till they reach the air. It is proved by experiment that an intervening vacuum stands in the way of sound-perception. The imaginary ether is in the vacuum, yet the sound is cut off. Ether does not help the propagation of sound. How may, therefore, ether (*ākāsha*) be accepted to be a source of sound-perception?

That sound-perception is stimulated by and through solids (*kshiti*), liquids (*ap*) and gases (*vāyu*) is not denied by the Hindu *Shāstras*, inasmuch as these, being modifications of ether, retain its property. So far their findings are on a par with those of modern science. It is regarding ether only that they hold a different opinion. A little scrutiny may show that their findings about ether do not really negate those of modern science, but only present an additional knowledge about it.

The sound which is commonly audible to us is produced and propagated by grosser matter[1] and it may be said to be a gross variety of sound. For, the Hindus hold that there is a highly subtle variety of sound not audible to the common ear. Hence, according to the Hindu view also, so far as gross sound is concerned, a vacuum (containing ether) may stand in the way of its propagation.

The Hindu seers had certain empirical data that led them to the conclusion that ether stimulates a highly subtle variety of sound-perception. In a state of deep meditation one hears a sound known as the *anāhata dhwani*. This sound is very subtle and is audible when the mind becomes very calm and collected. It has nothing to do with any vibration of coarser matter. The stimuli that produce the *anāhata dhwani* are always present, for it is always audible by a keen and refined sense of hearing (*shrotra*) whenever the mind is in a state of deep concentration. The only possible medium through which its perception may be stimulated is ether

---

[1] It may be that sound is produced in every case by the ether component of gas (*vāyu*), liquid (*ap*) or solid (*kshiti*) and amplified by the grosser components, when it becomes audible to the common ear.

(*ākāsha*).[1] Perhaps the reference to the music of the spheres in Greek mythology might have been based on some such experience. The idea of logos (word), called *Sphota* by the Hindus, at the beginning of Creation also points to the possibility of the subtlest and all-pervasive medium ether (*ākāsha*) being the source and conveyer of that sound. For coarser matter at that stage was not in existence.

Then, the order of evolution from ether to earth also does not contradict any of the findings of science. Evolution of the universe, as science has been able to trace it so far, starts from the nebula, which is described as a gaseous substance radiating heat and light. The starting-point of the scientists, therefore, is a state when, according to Hinduism, both air and fire have come into existence.

The scientists hold that the process of planet-building starts with the separation of masses from the nebula and is followed by gradual condensation of the detached masses. It is to be noted that the gases (*vāyu*) condense first into liquid (*ap*) and then into solid (*kshiti*). This is also the order suggested by the Hindu idea of evolution.

The Hindu *Shāstras* start with *ākāsha* (ether) as the first manifested physical entity. Out of this comes *vāyu* (gases) and out of *vāyu* *agni* (heat and light phenomena). This portion obviously belongs

---

[1] The phenomenon of *ākāsha-vāni* (a voice from heaven), also called *daiva vāni* (heavenly voice) or *asharirini vāni* (incorporeal voice), is another instance to the point.

to the pre-nebular stage of Creation about which science is as yet silent. Before the nebula came into being, the question arises—whether the gaseous substance (*vāyu*) preceded heat and light (*agni*) or the reverse was the case. Ether might very well have evolved into the coarser gaseous substance which by friction might have produced heat and light. This does not go against reason and appears to be quite likely.

It is to be noted that just as gross *ākāsha* is the first manifested physical entity, gross *prāna* is the first manifested physical energy. It is by the action of this energy on ether (*ākāsha*) that the gaseous substance (*vāyu*) is produced, and by its action on the gaseous substance that fire comes into being; and so on it goes till we have the entire physical universe. Under the impact of this energy (*prāna*) ether, which is a very subtle homogeneous substance, might have evolved into a coarser gaseous substance (*vāyu*) consisting of molecules. Then by the action of *prāna* on *vāyu* its molecules might have been set into motion, giving rise to what we call the phenomena of heat and light (*agni*). There is, therefore, nothing absurd about the idea of *agni* evolving out of *vāyu*.

Then, the composition of the gross *bhutas* from the inert (*tāmasika*) portions of the *tanmātras* is also worth noticing. The gross *bhutas*, being the basis of material existence, have the principles of inertia predominant in them. The genesis appears to be quite appropriate. Through the *tāmasika* principle in *Prakriti* energy *(shakti)* puts· on the look of inert matter. Does it not fit in with the scientist's conception of an atom as 'bottled up radiant energy'?

It should also be noted that the Hindu seers had a clear idea of what we call evolution. Patanjall, the author of the *Yoga Sutras*, referred to it as '*jātyantara-parināma*', that is, transformation of one genus or species into another. They had a definite idea about its cause, for which modern science may be said to be still groping. They held that one genus or species has within it, potentially, whatever evolves out of it. It is already there in the causal state (*prakriti*) of a particular genus or species, and this flows out, as it were, to manifest newer forms, whenever circumstances combine to give it an outlet.[1] Water stocked on a high ground may be made to irrigate the grounds on lower and lower levels by simply opening suitable outlets. Such operations are done by the cultivators.[2] In this way suitable circumstances may be said to make an opening through which the potential energy (*prakriti*) within a genus or species rushes out, as it were, to compose newer forms, giving rise to a new genus or species.[3]

[1] Cf. *Yg. S.* IV. 2. '*Jātyantaraparināmah prakrityāpurāt*'.
[2] Cf. *ibid.* IV. 3.
[3] See *Sw. Viv.'s Comp. Wks.* Part I (fifth ed.) 291-293.

Hinduism holds that the whole process of *Srishti* out of *Avyakta*, from *Brahmā* down to the grossest and tiniest object, is one of evolution, and that it is made possible by the process of involution[1] during *Pralaya*. It should also be noted that at the back of this evolution lies, according to Hinduism, the Divine Will[2] as its supreme cause.

---

[1] *i.e.*, returning to the seed-state, as it were.
[2] See *infra* Chap. XVIII.

XVIII

BRAHMĀNDA (*continued*)

CAUSAL

We have seen that *Srishti* starts with the *ākāsha tanmātra* out of *Avyakta* as a sprout coming out of a seed. Is *Avyakta* a substance that is transformed into *ākāsha*? No, it is of the nature of energy (*shakti*). God is the only substance, the only Reality and *Avyakta* or *Prakriti* is His *Shakti*.

During *Pralaya* there was nothing with name and form, neither was then time, space or causation. Nor was it a complete void. For One existed alone with Its mysterious power.[1] Before *Srishti* all this was pure Existence, One without a second.[2] That thought, "May I become many, may I manifest Myself numerously."[3] He willed, "Let Me project worlds." And He projected these worlds.[4]

God (*Ishwara*) Himself wills and through His mysterious power He projects the universe out of Himself. In *Avyakta* is the potentiality of throwing out the infinite forms of nature, but behind each form the substance is none other than God Himself. However, *Avyakta* being His power, He is both the efficient and material cause of the universe. This

---

[1] Cf. *Ṛg. Vd.* X. 129. 1–2.　　[2] Cf. *Chh. Up.* VI. 2. 1.
[3] *Ibid.* VI. 2. 3; cf. *Tait. Up.* II. 6.　　[4] Cf. *Ait. Up.* I. 1. 1–2.

is what the Vedānta, the ruling creed of the Hindus, holds. The Sāmkhya, Nyāya, Vaisheshika, Chārvāka, Bauddha and Jaina schools have, however, different theories about Creation. The various schools of Hindu thought of this day accept, more or less, the Vedāntic view-point.

However, being the efficient and material cause of the universe, God by His own will and through His mysterious power becomes all this. He appears first as ākāsha, then appears to be further modified as vāyu, and this process goes on till He manifests Himself as Hiranyagarbha; and then through Hiranyagarbha He proceeds to manifest Himself as numerous worlds, gross and fine, as well as their various contents, sentient and insentient. So every object, gross or fine, sentient or insentient, from Brahmā up to the blade of grass, from the Brahmaloka up to this earth—everything is He under a garb of particular name and form projected by Him through His mysterious power.

Does He actually become modified as all these? Some Vedāntists say, 'Yes'. Just as all earthen pots are made of clay, all golden ornaments of gold and all steel implements of iron, so are the various contents of the universe made of Him as the material. As the foams, ripples and waves are modifications (parināma) of the sea-water, so are all these of Him. According to this school, God Himself has literally become this universe by His will and rules it from within as the *Antaryāmi*. This is what is known as *Parināmavāda* upheld by the Vishishtādvaita school. All the *Bhakti* cults of our day, particularly the Vaishnava ones, are more or less in line with this view-point.

The Advaita school of Vedānta, on the other hand, holds that it is not a case of actual transformation. *Brahman* is changeless and He remains so throughout eternity. The universe is not a real projection, but an apparent one (*vivarta*). He merely appears as all these. The names and forms through which He appears as distinct entities are illusory. They have no absolute existence. When through illusion we take a rope for a snake, the rope itself is not affected in any way by our vision. So also *Brahman* is not affected in the least by our illusory vision of the universe. It is only under a sort of hypnosis that we see the universe; when the spell is over, as in the *nirvikalpa samādhi*, everything melts into the Changeless *Brahman*, just as a lump of salt loses its identity in the sea-water.

The illusory names and forms are thrown out by His mysterious power known variously as *Avyakta*, *Prakriti*, *Māyā*. This power is of the nature of Nescience (*Avidyā*). It has two components, namely, *āvarani shakti* (the power that veils) and *vikshepa shakti* (the power that projects). The former hides the Reality and the latter makes It appear as something other than what It is by throwing out illusory names and forms. This mysterious power contains within itself the possibilities of projecting the infinite forms of the universe, just as a tiny seed contains those of a multibranched peepul tree (*ashwattha*). It is within this *Avyakta* that the desires, experiences and the fruits of actions of all the *jivas* of the previous cycle lie latent during Dissolution. and these determine the forms to be projected through *Avyakta* during the next cycle.

Thus, according to this school, the universe has only a relative (*vyāvahārika*) existence and not an absolute (*pāramārthika*) one. It exists so long as we are under the spell of Nescience (*Avidyā*). It ceases to exist as soon as one steps out of the spell and attains full knowledge of the Supreme Reality, that is, becomes one with It. This truth is declared by the *Shāstras* and confirmed by the realization of the seers. Just as the things and events seen in a dream vanish altogether and become meaningless when one wakes up, so does the universe with all its contents disappear when one finds the Real Self. One then becomes perfectly awakened (*prabuddha*) to what really exists, the Absolute. Compared with That, the universe is no more than a dream.

So long as one sees a dream, the dream-objects are intensely real. So also is the universe with all its contents to one under the spell of *Avidyā*. On awakening to Absolute Reality, however, all these have no value, no meaning, no existence. Thus the universe is existent in an apparent, illusory and relative (*vyāvahārika*) sense, and at the same time non-existent in an absolute (*pāramārthika*) sense. This is something like the vision of a snake in a rope, of a mirage in the desert, of a scene in a dream.

This being so, the names and forms on *Brahman* being illusory, that which throws out these forms and names, namely, *Avyakta* or *Māyā*, is also illusory. Like the universe, the power by which it is projected, namely, *Māyā*, is also neither absolutely existent nor non-existent. It is something indefinable ('*Sadasadanirvachaniyarupā*'). With the help of such an incomprehensible power, called *Māyā*, the universe is projected. By whom? By *Ishwara*, the Omniscient, Omnipotent Master of *Māyā*. He is the Magician, *Māyā* is His magic-spell, the universe is the illusion projected by Him on Himself as the only substantial background.

What are the various objects seen on a cinema screen made of? They are all made of light. The composition of water, fire, earth, plants, engines, living beings and all that we see on the screen, is light and light alone. Light varied by shade, that is, by absence of light, works up the entire illusion. The light itself behind the film in the cinematograph is one formless luminous emanation. If the film were not there, we would see nothing but a uniformly lighted screen, as we really see when the film is removed. The film does not allow free passage of the light; it allows portions to pass and holds back others. This interruption of the film gives rise to the shades, and limited by these shades, the light on the screen appears as numerous and diverse objects. Moreover, it is to be noticed that the illusion of the motion of the pictures on the screen is not due to any motion of the light. It is created solely by the rearrangement of shades due to the motion of the film. As the film moves, the passage of light through it is interrupted in newer ways. The light is steady, the shades vary from moment to moment, and this is all that gives rise to the illusory moving scenes on the screen.

The illusion of the universe is wrought almost like this. God is like the light of the cinematograph and *Māyā* is like the moving film. Through *Māyā*, God appears to be diversified and concretized by infinite shades of names and forms, though really He does not undergo any change. If, in the cinema, the screen itself were nothing but light, and if it had within itself the power of diversifying itself by shades, then the analogy would be complete. For God throws the illusion of the universe on Himself as the background by His power *Māyā*. *Māyā* hides His reality and makes Him appear as the universe simply by working up infinite shades of names and forms. The names and forms are as unsubstantial as the shades on the screen.

Let us stretch the analogy a little further. If any

of the spectators want to trace the source of the illusory scene on the screen, what will he do? He will surely turn his back on the scene and proceed towards the projecting machine. Reaching that he will realize the combination of the film and the light behind as the cause of the illusion. So have countless seers, turning their back on the illusory universe, traced its cause to the Omniscient and Omnipotent *Parameshwara* with His mysterious power *Māyā*.

Some went a step further, when *Māyā* with her infinite shades of names and forms disappeared altogether and there was nothing but one Existence without name, form or attribute. This is the Supreme and the only Absolute Reality, One without a second, that appears as *Parameshwara* when associated with *Māyā*. That is, so long as we are in *Avidyā* and consequently see the universe, the Absolute Reality (*Parabrahman*) appears as *Parameshwara* endowed with the mysterious power *Māyā*, projecting, directing and controlling the illusion of the universe.

This, in short, is how the Advaita school of Vedānta explains *Srishti*. The change and no change of *Brahman* are explained by the analogies of dream and illusion. But *Māyā*, by which this is explained, is said to be neither real nor unreal, indefinable. It is absolutely incomprehensible. We can never comprehend such a combination of opposites, just as we can never conceive of simultaneous change and no change of *Brahman*. To rationalize one paradox, have we not taken recourse to another? Is not the mystery of *Srishti* still beyond our grasp?

Yes, by the very nature of things it is bound to remain so for ever. The Divine urge for *Srishti* and the first step towards it must remain an eternal mystery. These are not events of the order of natural phenomena; for at that stage there was neither time, nor space, nor causation. They were yet to come into existence. The question why or how of such things cannot arise. The Absolute is beyond the range of our mind and speech; so also must necessarily be the first stirrings for *Srishti*.

The *Rig-Veda* points to the inscrutable nature of the mystery of *Srishti* when it says, "Who knows thoroughly, who can describe with precision whence this manifold Creation has proceeded? Even the gods appeared after *Srishti*; so who knows whence it came?"[1] Evidently none. The fact that the Lord by His will projected all this out of Himself is revealed through the *Shāstras* and realized by the seers. Mere ratiocination will lead us nowhere, since this fact is beyond the scope of our understanding. Our thoughts may stagger at the idea of the eternally Changeless One becoming the basis of the ever-changing myriad-faced universe. Yet it

[1] *Rg. Vd.* X. 129. 6.

is so. We have to accept it as a fact. It can never be explained by human logic. The why and how of *Srishti* can never be traced by the human intellect. This fact that baffles our understanding by presenting the opposites is *Māyā*, as Swāmi Vivekānanda has put it. It is possible for Him to remain eternally perfect and changeless and yet to project, sustain and dissolve the universe at His will. Such is His inscrutable nature (*Prakriti*). Such is His mysterious power (*Shakti*). We need not bother about the why or how.

The truth about Srishti may, however, be realized by reaching the Lord. By knowing Him everything in creation becomes known, all riddles are solved. The aim of the different systems of religious thought within Hinduism is to lead their followers towards such realization. The different versions of the indescribable mystery of *Srishti* held out by them fit in with the different approaches to such realization prescribed by them. None of these can possibly present the whole truth about the transcendental mystery of *Srishti*. Yet each has the pragmatic value of drawing a section of humanity having a particular taste and capacity of understanding towards the realization of God. In this sense none is incorrect or useless.

XIX

JIVA

SOUL

A LIVING BEING

We have come across the word '*jiva*' on several occasions in the course of the previous topics. Already we have had some idea of what it stands for. Let us now go into further details.

The word '*Jiva*' literally means a living being. Whatever in nature possesses life is, in a broad sense, called a *jiva*. And the Hindu idea of nature as an abode of living beings is rather extensive. There are numerous worlds, gross and fine, for the *jivas* to live in. Thus a *jiva* may be an amoeba, a plant, an animal, a man or a deity (*devatā*). Even the topmost deity, *Hiranyagarbha*, as we have noted already, is a *jiva*. While referring to all *jivas* in creation, a very common expression used by the Hindu *Shāstras* is 'from *Brahmā* right up to a clump of grass.'[1] Indeed the *Brahmānda* comprising numerous worlds is conceived of as an abode of an infinite variety of living beings.

The *jivas* may be either *chara* (capable of moving about) or *achara* (incapable of doing that). According to the findings of the Hindu *rishis*, every *jiva*,

[1] '*Ā-brahma-stamba-paryantam*'.

chara or *achara*, be it a plant,[1] an animal, or a deity,
is sentient. Whatever has life has consciousness as
well. The difference between a plant and an animal
is in the degree of consciousness possessed by them.
Every *jiva* is a conscious entity and is subject to the
sensations (*vedanā*) of pain and pleasure. It is the
subject of experience as well as of action (*bhoktā* and
kartā). These are the outstanding features of a *jiva*,
and to these the entire mechanism of the universe
stands vitally related.

We have seen how its action is linked up with
its experience by the rigorous law of *karma*. Whatever a *jiva* has to experience in the shape of pain or
pleasure, is the sure result of some of its own deeds
performed during previous births. For reaping
the fruits of their action they go from birth to birth.
Even during Dissolution (*Pralaya*) the *jivas* remain
in a latent state, and it is for the fruition of their
past deeds that a fresh *Srishti* takes place, the
universe is projected. They really hold the centre
of the stage; everything else in nature is meant for
their action and experience.

The creatures (*jivas*) vary from one another not
only in names and forms but also in the powers of
knowledge and action. This power possessed by the
highest among them, namely *Hiranyagarbha*, is
unlimited, while that of an amoeba may very well
be said to be atomic. Even man with his limited

[1] '*Antahsamjnā bhavantyete sukhaduhkhasamanwitāh.*'

power of knowledge and action appears to be infinitely superior to an amoeba as far as this power is concerned. The immeasurable range between a man and an amoeba on this earth is actually found to be filled up by countless varieties of *jivas*. Similarly the gap between a man and *Hiranyagarbha* (*Brahmā*) being immeasurable, it is not unlikely that this also is filled up by countless varieties of *jivas*. The Hindu *Shāstras* hold that it is actually so; there are numerous orders of superhuman beings living outside this world.

There is nothing preposterous about it. The findings of the *Shāstras* are based on actual observation. That we do not ordinarily see such beings is no proof against their existence. We do not see the microbe as well. Yet the microbe is no myth. For we can see it under the microscope. So also we can observe these superhuman beings through *yogic* vision. Just as we are required to take pains for preparing a microscope, so also we have to strive for developing the powerful and clarified vision of a *yogi*. However, the fact of the existence of these beings rests on such observation and is, therefore, no myth.

These *jivas* who range between man and *Brahmā* inhabit various worlds other than this. The inhabitants of each of these worlds form a class by themselves bearing a common name. Some of these classes mentioned by the Hindu *Shāstras* are:

Yaksha, Sādhya, Kinnara, Gandharva and *Deva.* Mention is made also of further subdivisions, particularly of the last two,[1] each occupying a world of its own. However, it seems that the list of the superhuman *jivas* is only selective and not exhaustive.

This appears to be true also with regard to the list of the different worlds inhabited by these *jivas.* This world, *Prithivi,* is described to lie in the middle; above and below it many other worlds are said to exist. The *Brahmānda* comprising these three regions, the higher, the middle and the nether, called respectively *Swarga, Martta* and *Pātāla,* is also referred to as *Tribhuvana* (three worlds). A more detailed list mentions, however, fourteen worlds (*chaturdashabhuvanāni*). From this world upwards there are said to be seven, namely, *Bhuh, Bhuvah, Swar, Jana, Maha, Tapas* and *Satya*; and below this world there are seven, namely, *Atala, Vitala, Sutala, Rasātala, Talātala, Mahātala* and *Pātāla.*[2] In one of the Upanishads the seven higher worlds are mentioned as *Agniloka, Vāyuloka, Varunaloka, Ādityaloka, Indraloka, Prajāpatiloka* and *Brahmaloka.*[3] These may not correspond to the higher worlds on the previous list, but refer to some other distinct *lokas.* In any case the highest ones on the two lists, *Satyaloka* and *Brahmaloka,* are identical. Sometimes, however, the higher worlds are lumped under three heads, *Pitriloka, Devaloka* and *Brahmaloka.* None of the lists appears to be

[1] Cf. *Tait. Up.* II. 8. [2] Cf. *Ved. Sār.* 104. [3] Cf. *Kau. Up.* I. 3.

exhaustive; each suggests the existence of numerous subdivisions of the *Brahmānda*, of which few prominent ones are mentioned.

Another Hindu idea in this connection requires mention. Each of the worlds is said to be under a presiding deity (*adhishthātri-devatā*), and it is often named after the *devāta*. Thus the seven higher worlds on the second list indicate that they are respectively under the deities, *Agni*, *Vāyu*, *Varuna*, *Āditya*, *Indra*, *Prajāpati* and *Brahmā*. So are all other worlds under separate presiding deities.

Consciousness, according to Hinduism, is the eternal verity that pervades the whole universe. The subtle mechanism through which it is manifested in the inner nature is the *antahkarana* made of the fine *bhutas* (*tanmātras*). This also is all-pervasive, being none other than the body of the first cosmic being *Hiranyagarbha*. The gross physical mechanism through which actions are done also functions as one complete whole as the body of *Virāt*, and pervades the entire physical universe.

God appears first as *Hiranyagarbha*, then as *Virāt*, then He subdivides Himself into the various other deities and into all other *jivas*. This is how God becomes many by His *Māyā*. Each *jiva* is only a portion of *Virāt* with a distinct ego of its own. Just as innumerable cells live in the physical body of a man, so also do countless *jivas* in the all-pervasive body of *Virāt*. Such is the bold conception of the

Hindus. Indeed, Consciousness, the subtle mechanism of life and mind, as well as the gross physical
mechanism of action, all these three being held to be
all-pervading, any portion of nature surely contains
all that is necessary for the appearance of a *jiva*.

THE SOUL

A living being is a complex of sentient and insentient factors. It is the sentient principle in a
creature that is referred to by the *Shāstras* specifically
as the *jiva*.

Distinct from the mind, the sense-organs and
the physical body is the soul (*Ātman*), which is the
substantive part of a living being. It is the master of
the house. It is the rider on the chariot.[1] It is self-
effulgent (*antarjyotih*).[2] Consciousness is the essence
of its being. It alone is the sentient principle in the
make-up of a living being. And this, therefore, is
the *jiva per se*.

The soul is encased in three bodies ranging from
the grossest to the finest—the physical (*sthula*), the
subtle (*sukshma*) and the causal (*kārana*). The physical body is made of the gross *bhutas*, and the
subtle body of the *tanmātras* or subtle *bhutas*. This is
why these are said to be *bhautikas*, that is, made of
bhutas. The causal body is just a tiny portion of the
unmanifested Cosmic Energy, called *Avyakta*, of
which the *bhutas* and *bhautikas* are only manifested

[1] Cf. *Ka. Up.* I. 3. 3.   [2] Cf. *Bri. Up.* IV. 3. 7.

modes. *Avyakta* as also its modes are insentient; so, therefore, are all the three bodies, *sthula*, *sukshma* and *kārana*.

The causal body contains within itself all the characteristics and tendencies (*samskāras*) of a creature in the seed-state, as it were. As the seed is causally related to a tree, so is this body to the life and career of a creature. This is why it is said to be the causal body.

The fine body consists of, as we have seen in a previous chapter, three chambers—the *vijñānamaya*, *manomaya* and *prānamaya koshas*. These are the seats respectively of the functions of knowledge, cogitation and vitality. The first consists of *buddhi* (intellect) and the five sense-organs of knowledge, the second of the mind and the five sense-organs of knowledge and the third of the five *prānas* and the five organs of action. These are all subtle instruments of knowledge and action at the disposal of the *jiva*.

The physical body is built up by the *jiva* as determined by its actions and the resultant knowledge during previous births. This is why it is called *kārya* (effect) as distinct from the subtle body, which is called *karana* (instrument). The combination of these two is known as *kārya-karana-samghāta*. However, the instrument used in body-building is mainly the *prāna* (vital energy), which is really one, though enumerated commonly as five according to different functions. The *prāna* is directed by the *jiva* accord-

ing to the impressions (*samskāras*) stored in the
mind during previous births. The materials out of
which the physical body is built are gathered through
food from the world (*loka*) to which the *jiva* belongs
for the time. Through this gross physical body and
the organs the *jiva* comes in contact with the physical universe, and acts and reacts on the same.

All these three distinct bodies encasing the soul
are inanimate. The soul alone is sentient. It is referred to in the *Shāstras* as the radiant infinite being
who moves alone.[1] It is not a created entity like the
bhutas and *bhautikas*. God Himself appears as the
soul of a creature. The *Shāstras* announce, "He
created all this, whatever exists in the universe.
Having created that, He entered verily into that."[2]
Having projected the inanimate causal, subtle and
physical bodies of all creatures, big and small, God
is said to have entered them all as their soul. In the
Gitā the Lord says, "Verily it is a portion of Myself
that has become *jiva* (soul) in the world of living
beings."[3] This is why the soul (*jivātman* or simply
jiva) is said to be birthless, deathless, eternal and
so on.[4] The *jiva* (soul) is verily *Brahman* (the
Supreme Self) and none other than That. 'Verily
this great *Ātman* (soul) who is subject neither to
birth, decay nor death, is the Immortal *Brahman*
free from all fears.'[5]

---

[1] Cf. *ibid*. IV. 3. 11.   [2] *Tait. Up.* II. 6.   [3] *Gitā* XV. 7.
[4] Cf. *Ka. Up.* I. 2. 18.   [5] *Bri. Up.* IV. 4. 25.

From all such statements of the *Shāstras* the *Vishishtādvaita* (conditioned Non-dualism) school of Vedānta concludes that the soul is a real, eternally distinct particle, as it were, of God. As a spark is related to fire, so is *jiva* to *Ishwara*. It is essentially divine in its nature; only it is an infinitesimal portion of the Omniscient, Omnipotent and Omnipresent Lord. As a consequence of wicked deeds it becomes impure and then it is said to contract. Its essential divinity becomes suppressed for a while. But through suitable spiritual practice it gradually expands till it manifests its essential divinity completely. Then it becomes free to enjoy eternal bliss in the presence and company of God. This is more or less the idea of the *Bhakti* schools regarding the soul, its bondage and liberation.

The Advaita school of Vedānta, however, holds a different view. It declares that though the soul of an individual looks like a portion of the Great One, it is absolutely the same as the All-pervading 'Immortal *Brahman* free from all fears'. All the Upanishads teach such identity of the *jiva* and *Brahman*. This is why by knowing the *Ātman* as It really is one can become liberated. So long as the *jiva* considers itself, through ignorance (*avidyā*), just a tiny individual distinct from God and the rest of the universe, it remains bound. When, through suitable spiritual practice, it realizes its identity with the Supreme Self (*Paramātman*), then and then alone it becomes liberated from *samsāra*. Hence do the *Shāstras* enjoin, "The *Ātman* has to be realized; It has to be heard of, reflected about and meditated upon."[1]

The soul is none other than the Great One (*Parabrahman*) who alone is eternally present as the infinite ocean of Existence, Consciousness and Bliss. Everything else from *Avyakta* downwards has only a relative existence. They have their being only as long as the spell of ignorance (*avidyā*) lasts. On the dawning of Self-knowledge they vanish like a dream. And as long as they are observed to exist, they function only as an infinite series of material mediums, fine and gross, through which the same Universal Spirit (*Paramātman*) appears as myriads of distinct *jivas*. Each medium according to its structure gives a limited and coloured view of the same unbounded and formless Reality. This is why these mediums are called *upādhis*, that is, limiting adjuncts.

Through *Avyakta* (*Kārana*) as a whole as the *upādhi* the Great One appears as *Ishwara*, the Omniscient and Omnipotent Lord of Creation, Sustenance and Dissolution. At *Ishwara's* will and command *Avyakta* throws out subtle *upādhis* that lay within it in a latent state during *Pralaya*, and through these He appears as distinct *jivas*.

Through the veil (*upādhi*) of the cosmic intellect

[1] *Ibid*. II. 4. 5.

(*samashti buddhi*) He appears as *Hiranyagarbha*, and through that of the individual intellect (*vyashti buddhi*) He appears as any other being. Just as the same sun may appear to be many when seen through different pieces of variously coloured glasses, so the same Lord appears as myriads of distinct *jivas* through different veils of individual *buddhi*.

Buddhi (intellect) is the finest material instrument of knowledge and action. It occupies the chamber of knowledge (*vijnānamaya kosha*) of the subtle body (*sukshma sharira*), which is said to be lodged in the region covered by the heart (*hridaya*) and is reported to be of the size of an adult's thumb and like the physical body in appearance.

Though *buddhi* is by itself insentient, it has the property of being illumined by the all-pervading Consciousness of the Lord. Just as the moon made luminous by the sun appears like an independent luminary, so does *buddhi* at the touch of the all-pervading Consciousness of the Lord appear to be a distinct conscious being with an ego of its own. The source of consciousness is none other than God Himself. *Buddhi* shines only in borrowed sentience. It catches, as it were, a reflected image of the Lord.

An image, as we know, is only an illusion caused by the reflection of light. A replica of the original source of light is seen within the reflecting medium, and that is called an image. A sheet of water, for instance, reflects the sun's rays, that is, turns the course of the rays in a different direction. This produces an impression that the rays are coming straight from the water. In that direction within the sheet of water we see a replica of the sun. This illusory facsimile of the sun is what we call its image. The image of the Lord in *buddhi* is such an illusory phenomenon.

Brahman is all-pervading, eternally steady and absolutely changeless Consciousness. The intellect (*buddhi*), which is absolutely insentient, reflects, as it were, a portion of His Consciousness. This produces a false impression that within *buddhi* itself there is a distinct, tiny source of Consciousness. This illusory tiny source of Consciousness in *buddhi* is said to be the image of the Lord. As a matter of fact it is reported by the *Shāstras* to be atomic in size.[1] Really the Infinite Lord has not split Himself into myriads of atomic souls and lodged Himself separately within the minute *vijñānamaya kosha* of every creature. He only appears as so many minute and distinct souls through distinct individual intellects, just as the same sun appears to be many through its images on different sheets of water.

It is this image of the Lord, this borrowed Consciousness of the intellect, that is the only sentient principle in the structure of a living being. It is the *jivātman*, the *jiva per se*. It is this image of the Lord to which the ego of a creature immediately

[1] *Esho'nurātmā.—Mund. Up.* III. 1. 9.

points. It is what a man refers to when he says 'I'. This is the *Ātman*, 'the Infinite One who identifying Itself with the intellect lives within the heart as the self-effulgent entity in the midst of the sense-organs.'[1]

Everything else in the structure of a creature from the intellect (*buddhi*) outwards is its instrument. They are all insentient by themselves. They appear to shine as conscious entities only owing to their contact with the soul. Just as a piece of iron put in fire becomes red-hot and looks like fire itself when it begins to radiate heat and light, so also the intellect, the mind, the sense-organs and even the physical body, by their contact with the soul, look like conscious entities.

When the instruments are thus illumined by the soul with its consciousness, they start functioning. The intellect (*buddhi*) being the subtlest of the inner instruments (*antahkarana*) is illumined first by the all-pervading Consciousness of the Lord. This is why it is said to hold the image of the Lord within itself. However, thus illumined, it starts functioning as the subject of action and experience. But by illusion Consciousness itself as reflected by the intellect appears to be functioning in this way. Just as the sun remains steady, yet its image in a sheet of water may be seen to be dancing with the waves on the surface, so also although *Brahman* as All-

[1] *Bri. Up.* IV. 3. 7.

pervading Consciousness remains eternally steady, Its illusory image in the intellect as the soul appears to be moving and functioning when the intellect is really doing that. It does neither act nor experience. It only appears to do so owing to Its illusory identification with the intellect. This is why the soul is described as *vijnānamaya*. Yet by itself the soul as Consciousness is none other than God Himself, animating the intellect and standing apart as the Eternal Witness of everything during the states of waking, dream and sound sleep.

Thus within the same body there appear to be two entities, namely, the intellect animated by and identified with the soul as the subject of action and experience and the soul purely as the witness. These two, the acting and experiencing self (*jiva*) and the Witness Self (*Ishwara*), are described in the Upanishads by a beautiful imagery. They are represented as a couple of birds of the same name perching on the same tree in close union with each other, one of them eating savoury fruits and the other merely looking on.[1] They are also referred to as darkness and light residing within the same intellect.[2]

However, the soul identified with the intellect is the *jiva*. Like the active bird on the tree, he tastes the bitter and sweet fruits of his own action in the

---

[1] Cf. *Mund. Up.* III. 1. 1; also cf. *Shwet. Up.* IV. 6.
[2] Cf. *Ka. Up.* I. 3. 1.

shape of pain and pleasure. He animates the rest of the inner instruments (*antahkarana*), namely, the mind, the *prānas* and the subtle organs of knowledge and action, as well as the entire physical body.

Through the physical body and the sense-organs the soul of a man contacts the external world. Propelled by desires, it performs various deeds, good and bad, and thereby earns merits (*punya*) and demerits (*pāpa*) that are sure to come back to it in the shape of pleasure and pain in some future birth. Thus its life in *samsāra* goes on lengthening and drags it through repeated births. This has been going on eternally in the beginningless career of every *jiva*. And this will continue as long as the intellect will last to hold the image of the Lord within it as the individual soul (*jivātman*). The intellect disappears only on the dawning of Self-knowledge. Till then the *jiva* is bound to *samsāra*. This is why it is referred to as darkness as compared with its intrinsic luminous nature as God. This is also why the physical body and the sense-organs, which relate it to the external world and subject it to actions and their results, are described in the *Shāstras* as evils (*pāpmānah*)[1] and also as forms of death (*mrityo rupāni*).[2]

The body and sense-organs become active, however, only in the waking state. It is then only that the soul comes in contact with the outer world.

[1] Cf. *Bri. Up.* IV. 3. 8.　　　　[2] Cf. *ibid.* IV. 3. 7.

This state, therefore, presents the *jiva* in a distinct phase. It then identifies itself with the entire machinery of mind and body. Consciousness (*Brahman*) during this state appears to be veiled and coloured by all the three bodies, causal, subtle and physical. This particular phase of the *jiva* during the waking state is marked out by the *Shāstras* by a special name, *Vishwa*. It is an infinitesimal portion of the cosmic being called *Vaishwānara* or *Virāt*.

In the dream-state it releases itself from the grip of the physical body and the sense-organs, and thus breaks its contact with the outer world. With certain mental impressions (*samskāras*) carried from its experiences during the waking state as materials, it creates by its own light a dream-body and a mental world of its own and behaves therein as the subject of action and experience.[1] Consciousness during this state of dream is veiled and coloured by two bodies only, the causal and the subtle. This state presents another phase of the *jiva* known as *Taijasa*. It corresponds to *Hiranyagarbha* on the cosmic scale.

In the state of sound sleep (*sushupti*), the intellect (*buddhi*) as such ceases to exist and function. It becomes reduced to the causal state. Its relation, however, to the soul continues in a latent condition.[2] The causal body (*kārana sharira*) then remains as the only cover of Consciousness. This body, as we

[1] Cf. *ibid.* IV. 3. 9.   [2] Cf. *Br. S.* II. 3. 31.

have already seen, is of the nature of unmanifested potential energy (*avyakta*), containing within itself the possibilities of the *jiva* in a seed-state, as it were. It has no movement, no action. Even the restless senses, mind and intellect rest quietly in the causal state within this body. The only function of this body is to veil full Self-knowledge.

Yet during sound sleep the Reality veiled only by the causal body, which is also called the chamber of bliss (*ānandamaya kosha*), appears very much like Its own Being of Consciousness and Bliss. During this state the soul remains at rest, as it really is always. It is no longer swayed by the movement of the mind and body. It simply witnesses the state and fills it with peace by its own bliss. 'As a hawk or a falcon when tired of flying in the sky stretches its wings and becomes bound for its nest, so does the infinite being run for this state, where falling asleep he cherishes no desires and sees no dreams.'[1] Thus does the soul, tired of its actions and experiences during the waking and dreaming states, come to its own state of rest in sound sleep. This is why in this state the *jiva* is said to be united with the Reality.[2] The Sanskrit word *swapiti*, corresponding to the verb 'sleep' in the third person singular, is said to suggest that one comes to one's real Self during this state (*Swam apito bhavati*).[3]

The soul, however, does not appear to perceive

[1] *Bri. Up.* IV. 3. 19.   [2] Cf. *Chh. Up.* VI. 8. 1.   [3] *Ibid.* VI. 8. 1.

or know anything during sound sleep. It looks like that only because during that state there does not remain a second object outside itself to be perceived or known.[1] Its consciousness being indestructible remains unaffected all the while. On awakening it remembers that it had an undisturbed sleep. This also proves the continuity of the witnessing function of the soul during *sushupti*.

However, Consciousness in this state, veiled and coloured only by the causal body, manifests a distinct phase of the *jiva's* life and experience. This fact is emphasized by the Hindu *Shāstras* by marking out the *jiva* in this state by a special name, namely, *Prājna*. When the Supreme Reality (*Parabrahman*) is veiled and coloured by the individual causal body, That appears as *Prājna*, and when veiled and coloured by the cosmic causal body, That appears as *Ishwara*.

Thus the *jiva* passes alternately through the three different states of waking, dream and sound sleep. Each state presents it in a particular phase. In the waking state its action and experience are related to the physical universe, in the dream-state to a mental world created by itself, and in sound sleep it only witnesses the state of perfect rest and experiences bliss. It should be noted that the *jiva* as *vijnānamaya* (identified with the intellect) functions only in the first two states as *Vishwa* and *Taijasa*. In

[1] Cf. *Bri. Up.* IV. 3. 23.

the third state its *jivahood* remains dormant; freed from the intellect (which is then reduced to the causal state), the soul appears to become one with God (*Ishwara*) as *Prājna* and rests purely as witness.

This is why it is stated in the *Shāstras* that the *jivātman*, the self-effulgent one identified with the intellect, moves over and over again between the waking and dream states by making and breaking contact with the physical body and the sense-organs. It moves freely between these two states like a gigantic fish moving alternately between the two banks of a river unimpeded by its currents.[1]

Exactly in a similar way the *jiva* moves alternately between this world and the next[2] by coming into and going out of a particular physical body. In any physical body the soul lives for a time determined by a portion of the results of its previous actions. This portion of its *karmaphala* that determines its present life is called *prārabdha*. When it is spent up, the soul with the causal and subtle bodies leaves the physical body. This phenomenon is called death. It is really the gross body that dies, and not the soul. 'Bereft of the *jiva* (soul), this (body) dies, the *jiva* does not die.'[3] It is only in a figurative sense that the soul is popularly said to be born when it comes to possess a physical body, and to die when it leaves the same.[4] Really, the soul is not subject

---

[1] Cf. *ibid.* IV. 3. 18.　　[2] Cf. *ibid.* IV. 3. 9.
[3] *Chh. Up.* VI. 11. 3.　　[4] Cf. *Bri. Up.* IV. 3. 8.

to birth, growth or decay; all these changes come upon the physical body only.

As a matter of fact it is the subtle body that passes out of the physical one, carrying the image of the Lord as its soul. The Lord as Consciousness Itself is All-pervading and has, therefore, nowhere to move. It is only His illusory image in the intellect that appears to move with the latter. In this sense only the soul is said to be born when, illumined by its lustre, the intellect with the other inner instruments enters a gross body, and is said to die when the same goes out of it.

Thus the *jiva* moves between this world and the next. Its career through births and deaths is said to have had no beginning in time. The causal and subtle bodies last through cycles of Creation and Dissolution (*kalpa*). Nothing in nature can destroy them. They disappear, as we have said, only on the dawning of Self-knowledge. As long as the soul looks like the intellect and the intellect like the soul, these two bodies persist. Primal Ignorance (*Avidyā*) creates this illusion. The properties of one appear to be belonging to another. This illusion is technically called *adhyāsa*. Even the entire combination of body and mind poses as a conscious entity like the soul owing to this *adhyāsa*. This is why a man says, "I am old, I am sick, I am worried, I am happy", when really the physical body or the mind is so affected.

This illusion (*adhyāsa*) disappears when man realizes his Self, as It really is. It is then and then only that the beginningless career of a *jiva* comes to a glorious end. *Māyā* and its illusory progeny of names and forms vanish altogether. All limiting adjuncts (*upādhis*) drop off. Nothing remains to cover and colour the Supreme Reality, nothing to reflect Consciousness and hold Its image. What had been, through countless cycles of Creation and Dissolution, considering itself through *Māyā* as a *jiva* with limited powers of knowledge and action finds itself at long last as none other than the Supreme Reality, the infinite ocean of Existence, Consciousness and Bliss. Just as a river after coursing through various tracts at last reaches the sea and loses its separate existence in the same, so does the *jiva* after its beginningless journey through innumerable births and deaths in various worlds with diverse bodies at last reach its Great Source and become merged in That. Thus does the dream of the *jiva*'s career come to an end when it comes to know who it really is.

Man is so placed that it is possible for him to reach this goal through complete Self-knowledge. Some succeed in the attempt in this life and become what is known as *jivanmukta* (liberated while living). Some attain it at the end of this life (*videha-mukti*). Some others make substantial progress during this life, and proceed after death towards the goal through what is called the path of gradual liberation (*krama-mukti*). After death they are said to pass through various higher worlds till they reach the *Brahmaloka*, where they live till the end of the cycle and then become liberated with *Hiranyagarbha*, the presiding deity of that world.

All others who, goaded by desire, perform good or evil deeds go for a while to the higher or nether worlds and come back to this earth. For reaping the fruits of their actions they may even have to be born as plants, insects or lower animals. After they have suffered the consequences of their evil deeds through such lower lives, they are born again as men. It is as man only that the *jiva* gets the chance of attaining Self-knowledge and becoming free. This is why the human life is highly extolled by the *Shāstras* as an exceptionally privileged position for the *jiva* to manifest the Divinity within it.

XX

RITUALS AND MYTHOLOGY

THE previous chapters acquaint us with the spiritual truths underlying Hinduism. These form what may be said to be the core of the religion. The rest are mere externals meant for bringing these truths home to people. Rituals and mythology are such externals.

The spiritual truths, as we have seen, are highly abstruse. It is very difficult to grasp their import even with a fine intellect. Moreover, mere intellectual grasp of these does not take one very far in the spiritual realm. To quote the Scriptures or to talk glibly on religious topics is not the end in view. For spiritual growth, one has not only to understand these truths but also to govern one's life and conduct in their light till the truths are realized. Such realization is the goal to be attained. This can be had only through a pure heart. One's mind has to be thoroughly cleansed before this is possible.

Such purification of the mind develops a powerful faculty, namely, the intuition of a pure heart. And it is through this faculty that the spiritual truths are realized. The truths about God, nature and soul flash across the intuition of a pure heart. All experiences dubbed as supernatural or supernormal come through this faculty. Everyone is endowed with intuition; only it remains clouded in an unclean mind. This is why it does not function effectively till the mind is purified. When brightened up, it serves as the gate of knowledge *par excellence*. The subtler and higher verities that lie beyond the range of our senses (*atindriya*) and intellect reach our consciousness direct through this gate.

When this faculty is so developed, then alone man may be said to have attained his full stature. Then alone he should be described as a normal man and his vision as normal vision. The knowledge of subtler and higher realities obtained through the intuition of a pure heart is based on the normal and natural experience of a full-grown man. Those who have not developed this faculty should more correctly be dubbed as subnormal. Compared with the intellectual man, the savage belongs to a subnormal stage of human existence; so also, compared with the man of pure intuition, the man of mere intellect may very well be said to be in a subnormal stage of human development.

However, this faculty, through which the higher truths are realized, is developed only when the mind is purified. This is why the sole business of practical religion is to help the cleansing of one's mind. For then realization will naturally follow. And herein lies the utility of both rituals and mythology.

RITUALS

From the beginning to the end, the Hindu rituals are meant for purifying the mind. They seem to have no other object in view.

Of course, certain unedifying rituals that may very well be classed as magic rites have been in vogue since the days of the *Atharva-Veda* and prescribed in later days by the Tantras. These rites are intended either for crushing one's foe or for gaining a coveted object, for curing maladies or for averting misfortunes. So long as the end in view has the sanction of the *Shāstras*, these rites practised by the people on the *Pravritti Mārga* are not harmful. The foe, for instance, may be an antisocial element, who has to be crushed for the well-being of the society. The coveted object may not be an unworthy one. In such cases the practice of even these magic rites cannot degrade one spiritually. But these are likely to be abused by unclean and weak minds. They may easily be tempted to take to these rites for gaining some selfish and nefarious ends. Herein lurks the danger of spiritual degradation.

Leaving aside such rituals, all others are conducive to spiritual well-being. They go to chasten one's mind, and this, we have already seen, is an inevitable step towards the realization of God. But how may rituals help to purge the mind of its impurities? Let us see how.

We have learnt in a previous chapter that the

root-cause of all mental impurities is the ignorance about our essential divinity. Anything that reduces this ignorance certainly goes to purify the mind. Contemplation on God and the divinity of our soul goes to eliminate ignorance, and is, therefore, an effective purifier of the mind. Abstract contemplation, however, is a very stiff job beyond the capacity of many. But it becomes easy enough for all when it is made concrete through rituals.

The use of images and symbols to represent God is an instance to the point. All the while one worships before an image (*pratimā*) or a symbol (*pratika*), one is surely thinking of God and none else. This switching off of one's thoughts Godward is the greatest purifier, and it comes so easily when one tries to feel Divine presence through a concrete form. It cannot but be hard even for an intellectual man to keep his mind pitched up for long to the thought of the Infinite, Formless Lord of the universe.

The process of vitalizing an image (*prāna-pratishthā*) referred to in a previous chapter[1] shows clearly how rituals can help the gradual assimilation of the idea of the divinity of the soul. The devotee has to think that God emerges in a particular luminous form out of his soul within the heart, comes out of him with his breath and is then conveyed through a flower to the image, when the

[1] Chap. XII.

latter is said to come to life. The process may appear to be rather childish to the intellectuals. Yet like a kindergarten exercise, it is highly effective even to the intellectuals, most of whom are no more than infants so far as their spiritual growth is concerned. Through repeated performance of this, one becomes gradually aware of the divinity of the soul.

The thoughts about the immanence of God in nature also work through rituals as potent purifiers of the mind. By such thoughts the devotee's mind is transported for a while above the sordid context of the world. Everything in nature together with his own body and mind is deified as a necessary pre-condition for worshipping God and holding communion with Him.[1]

God manifests Himself as nature. This is one of the outstanding spiritual truths preached by Hinduism. When one's mind becomes absolutely clean, one realizes this. He actually sees God everywhere and in everything. But before such a vision is possible, one has to strive hard to rub in this truth, as it were, through intense thinking on it and its implications. The more he thinks about it, the more does his mind move away from ignorance and consequent impurities. The Hindu rituals provide ample opportunities for intensifying such thoughts in an easy and interesting way.

Just as a working knowledge of the abstract

---

[1] 'Devo bhutwā devam yajet'.

ideas about the numerals as well as about the simple arithmetical process (of addition, subtraction, etc.) may be imparted to a child with the help of a number of beads, so also the highly abstract idea of God's immanence in nature may be instilled in a way into crude minds with the help of concrete objects.

This is done by singling out natural objects and regarding the same as holy. An entire mountain range, for example—the Himālaya or the Vindhya, has to be looked upon as a holy thing. The sea is another holy object. So also are several rivers, such as the Ganges, the Jumnā, the Godāvari, the Saraswati, the Narbadā, the Indus (Sindhu) and the Kāveri. The rivers and mountains are the bodies of their presiding deities who are worshipped by the Hindus. These deities are superior manifestations of God.

Even cities or villages like Vārānasi, Allāhābād, Hardwār, Vrindāvan, Ayodhyā, Dwārkā, Puri, Ujjain, Kānchipuram, Rāmeshwaram and Kanyākumāri are all holy places for pilgrims to resort to. The atmosphere of these places is congenial to realization. All-pervading God appears to be thinly veiled, as it were, in these areas, so that a little search may lead one up to Him. Everyone is warmed up spiritually by the almost manifest Divine Presence. This is why the very dust on the streets of these places is said to be holy.

Then certain trees, herbs, grass, wood, flowers, leaves, metals, stones, etc. are considered holy. And this is not all. In the course of worship, the goddess *Durgā* has to be bathed in water drawn from various sources or mixed with scores of things, which are all considered holy. The idea behind all this is to extend the devotee's vision of holiness to every corner of the world. Nothing really is unholy. Some of the rituals require one to regard the earth, the sun, the moon, the planets and the stars as sacred objects, being the physical bodies of their presiding deities. In fact, the rituals help one to regard everything in nature as a holy object. This thought of all-pervading holiness sanctifies one's own mind, purges it of evil propensities and makes it gradually fit for realizing the Divine immanence in nature.

In this connection a word about the worship of God as *Shiva* through the symbol (*pratika*) of the *linga* will not be out of place. Some moderners are apt to sneer at it as a survival of the savage rite of phallic worship. It might have been a phallic rite at the origin, just as the Eucharist ceremony of the Christians might have had a cannibalistic origin. That does not matter in the least. For it has been sublimated into something far remote from the original rite. The suggestion of the phallus has been dropped altogether. The *Shiva-linga* stands for a holy emblem of God as *Shiva*—the word *linga* primarily meaning a symbol. Through it one worships God Himself, thinks of Him alone and nothing else. Such contemplation of God certainly goes to purify one's mind. This shows how far the daring Hindus could go on the strength of their conviction regarding the Divine immanence in nature. Even the phallus—supposing this interpretation is correct[1]—has been deified by them and converted into an aid to one's spiritual growth!

Besides contemplation of God, His immanence in nature and the divinity of the soul, thoughts about the purity of the devotee's own body and mind and of everything about him form what may be said to be the psychological background of all Hindu rituals. Such thoughts of purity check for the time being all unclean thoughts and impulses and thus induce the mind into a mood for holy communion. This mood has to be worked up before the devotee takes up the ceremony of actual worship. Everything else from the beginning is only a preliminary self-purifying process meant for lifting the mind to such a holy mood.

A few instances from the ritual connected with ordinary *Tāntrika* worship may illustrate this point. Before going in for worship, the devotee has to bathe, preferably in some holy water, cleanse his body thoroughly and then put on a clean suit of

---

[1] For another interpretation see *Sw. Viv.'s Comp. Wks.* Vol. IV (fourth ed.), pp. 357–58.

clothes often set apart for this purpose. The place of
worship must have a holy association; it may be
within a temple or under a sacred tree or in the
shrine attached to one's household. In any case
the place together with all articles to be used in
connection with that worship have to be scrupu-
lously cleaned. Before proceeding to the place, the
devotee is to turn his mind towards God through
contemplation, hymns and repetition of His holy
name (*japa*).

Just before entering its precincts he is to pray
for getting his mind purged of all impurities. Then
inviting some deities to witness his worship, he is
to purify himself by what is called *āchamana*. The
sacred formula (*mantra*) recited in this connection
is interesting, its purport being, 'Sages constantly
visualize the highest state of the Lord (*Vishnu*) like
eyes stretched in the sky'. Instilling faith in *Parabrahman* as the Ultimate Reality is evidently the
purpose of this sacred formula, and this is held as
an effective means of self-purification.

Then he purifies the water to be used in worship
by inviting the presiding deities of all the seven holy
rivers within it. After this, this water itself becomes
a purifying agent. With suitable sacred formulae
this water is sprinkled for purifying the accessories,
such as the devotee's seat, the flowers and their
containers, the incense-holder, the light-stand, the
offerings, in fact, everything connected with wor-

ship. The devotee has to purify even the floor
below his own seat with a sacred formula purport-
ing to be, 'O *Prithwi* (the presiding deity of this
earth), the people are held by thee, thyself art held
by the Lord (*Vishnu*), may thou hold me always and
purify this seat'. It shows how through such simple
things the vision is extended to the All-pervading
Divinity, and thereby the mind is elevated to a
higher plane.

Then the contemplation connected with the step
known as *bhuta-shuddhi* is highly interesting. It shows
how through concrete forms one's thoughts are led
step by step to the dissolution of the universe and
merging of the soul in *Parabrahman* and again to
their emergence in a deified form. In the course of
this process one had also to think of drying up and
then burning to ashes the body of personified evil
(*Pāpapurusha*) together with one's own subtle body,
and then of the generation of a fresh celestial subtle
body by nectar dribbling from the moon in the
forehead. Through these concrete forms the devotee
is induced to believe that his mind has become
spotlessly clean.

The thoughts may be allegorical, almost poetic;
but the effect produced by them is tangible. What
we intensely think we become. If we keep brooding
on our weakness and wickedness, weak and wicked
we remain. On the contrary, if we insist on thinking
that we are pure, pure we become. It is a kind of

14

self-hypnosis. We are essentially pure. Through Primal Ignorance we hypnotize ourselves to see in us sinners and behave as such. We have to dehypnotize ourselves by reversing the current of thoughts. And this is exactly the idea behind all the preliminary processes of self-purification connected with Hindu worship. Even the physical body, in fact, every point on it, is to be divinized through the process called *nyāsa*.

After all these are done, the devotee proceeds to worship God through an image or a symbol. The worship is a course of entertainment. The deity is welcomed, offered a seat, bathed and dressed, and then regaled with flowers, incense and dainty dishes. Thus divinizing himself by the preliminary processes of self-purification and humanizing the Divine through this course of entertainment, the devotee lives during the period of worship as close as possible to God in a mood of holy communion.

The entire course of entertainment, moreover, has to be repeated mentally. This is called *mānasa puja*. This helps the devotee to draw his mind away from the physical surroundings and remain absorbed in Divine contemplation, and that through the highly interesting concrete thoughts of mental worship. This is clearly a step ahead leading the devotee's mind from the gross to the subtle plane.

The process called *ārātrika* appears to emphasize the glory of the Lord after He has been entertained in a human way. This seems to be a symbolic worship. It consists of waving before the image of the Lord light, water, cloth, flower and the *Chamara*.[1] These appear to stand for the five elements (*bhutas*), namely, fire, water, ether, earth and air. The cloth[2] having numerous pores symbolizes ether; and smell being the special property of earth, the latter is best represented by a flower. The whole universe represented by its elementary constituents is thus offered symbolically to the Lord by way of His worship. What a majestic form of worship of the All-pervading One is prescribed for lifting up the devotee's mind from the humanized view of the Lord to the supercosmic view!

The ceremony is fittingly closed by the performance of what is called *homa*. This consists of oblations in a sacred fire lit for the purpose, and is obviously a survival of the Vedic form of worship. However, this rite at the close of the ceremony is significant. Hereby the devotee's idea of God is helped to transcend the limitation of the form imposed so long by the image, physical or mental. Through *Agni*, the presiding deity of fire, the offerings of the devotee are conveyed to the Lord of the universe. What is more, the devotee is sometimes required even to offer the universe together with its Creator, the Personal God (*Shiva*), by way of obla-

---

[1] A whisk made of the bushy tail of the yak.
[2] A synonym for which, *viz.*, *ambara*, means also the ether.

tion to the sacred fire.[1] What a bold ritual aimed at helping the devotee to transcend all forms and realize the identity of his soul with the Universal Spirit (*Parabrahman*)!

However, the above samples will suffice to show how the Hindu rituals aim at chastening the mind through an interesting and effective course of spiritual practice. If pursued earnestly and perseveringly and without any ulterior motive, they are sure to purify the mind more and more till the faculty of pure intuition is released to realize the higher spiritual truths.

MYTHOLOGY

Mythology aims at inspiring, through precepts and laudable examples, to strive to pitch up one's life to the highest ideal. It consists of stories, parables and legends, with or without any historical basis. Some of these are allegorical, some are full of poetic imagery, some are narrations of certain events of the legendary past. Through them all, however, the abstract and highly subtle ideas of Hinduism are successfully conveyed to the mass mind. The abstract teachings are made concrete, as it were, and rendered highly interesting and impressive through the garb of stories.

Such a technique was in use even as early as the days of the Vedic *Brāhmanas*. In the *Brāhmanas* are

[1] *Vishwam juhomi vasudhādi Shivāvasānam—Mnv. Tr.* Chap. V. foot-note.

found *Itihāsas* (myths and legends), *Purānas* (cosmogonic myths), *Gāthās* (epic song verses) and *Nārāsamsi* (songs in praise of heroes).[1] In course of time a distinct literature along this line grew up and swelled in volume comprising what is known as Hindu mythology.

The bulk of this literature may be classed as narrative poetry, some like the *Rāmāyana* and the *Mahābhārata* being of the order of epics. This is why it has been an admirable vehicle for conveying the lofty and abstract ideas and ideals of Hinduism straight to the heart of the masses. And it has been used in this way since the days of the Vedic *Brāhmanas*.[2] In those days the recital of narrative poems formed a part of religious ceremonies. Such recitals, for instance, had to be made everyday for a year as a necessary prelude to the great *ashwamedha yajna* (horse-sacrifice). Such poetry would also be recited or sung at the court of kings by a class of people known as *Sutas*, and even the hermits would assemble in a secluded place and spend the rainy season listening to the recitals of *Ākhyānas* (mythological narratives), *Itihāsas* and *Purānas*. Such a custom in some form or other has persisted even to our day. A religious or social function is very often attended by a dramatic presentation of a portion of Hindu mythology, or of recital and exposition of

---

[1] Vide *A History of Indian Literature* by Winternitz—Vol. I, p. 226.
[2] *Ibid.* p. 311.

the same by an expert known as *kathaka* (one who narrates). Thus through the ages the lofty ideas and ideals of Hinduism have been conveyed through impressive stories and inspiring historical facts to every stratum of the Hindu society.

This consistent and stupendous effort carried on at least through six thousand years for universal religious education among the Hindus is certainly a very striking phenomenon. It bespeaks highly of the wonderfully persevering zeal of the Hindus in matters concerning religion. And it has not been in vain. By this process through millenniums the mass mind has been thoroughly saturated with Hindu ideas and ideals. Though the highly abstract ideas may be beyond their reach, they are acquainted with some figurative versions of the same, which is enough to stir up their earnestness in religious pursuit. Illumined only by such knowledge of the *Shāstras*, some belonging to the lower strata of the Hindu society are often found to be inspired by the highest ideal of spiritual life. Really, mythology acts like a lever in lifting up the mass mind to spiritual heights.

Let us now have a peep into Hindu mythology and see how it works such miracles. In the first place, it presents the abstract Hindu ideas regarding God, soul and nature through concrete imagery. Just as information and instruction may be given through pictures, so they may be done through stories. Neither the picture nor the story is truth by itself, yet each helps to impress a truth on one's mind. What is a map? Surely it is not the country it represents, but it enables one to know a good deal about the land. This also is the case with the myths. These are not meant to be literally true, yet through them one may have some idea about the subtle metaphysical truths. Even as early as the days of the Vedas, specific directions were given as to how the *Ākhyānas* were to be interpreted instead of being taken to be literally true.

The story of Creation, for instance, which is a favourite and, in fact, an invariable theme of the mythological literature of India, particularly of the *Purānas*, will make the point clear. Let us take a version of this story.[1] *Nārāyana* (God), the Blue-bodied One with four hands in yellow robes, is lying still with closed eyes on a hydraheaded serpent (*Ananta Nāga*) floating on an all-pervading, fathomless sea. The waters of the boundless sea (*ekārnava*) are said to be *kārana salila* (causal water). Nothing else exists. This is the picture of *Pralaya*. On the eve of Creation, out of *Nārāyana's* navel springs a lotus flooding the entire sea with its lustre, and on this lotus appears *Brahmā*, the red deity with four faces and four hands. By the Lord's command *Brahmā* meditates on the past cycle (*kalpa*) and then proceeds to create the universe accordingly.

[1] Cf. *Bh. Pr.* III. 8.

What a splendid picture of an indescribable truth! The description of the state of *Pralaya* (Dissolution) in the *Rig-Veda* takes one's breath away. 'Neither naught nor aught existed at the time, neither heaven nor earth.... Neither was then death nor immortal life, there was nothing to distinguish between day and night. The One with Its power *Swadhā* alone breathed, though devoid of *prāna*; nothing else existed. Before Creation all this was darkness shrouded in darkness and remained merged in *kārana*. The universe that lay veiled by all-pervading but trivial ignorance (*Ajnāna*) during *Pralaya* became again manifested through names and forms by the Lord's will.'[1] It is interesting to note that the word '*salilam*' used in the Vedic text for *kārana* literally means water. This portion has actually been translated by a European scholar as 'far and wide an impenetrable flood'. However, the metaphorical use of the word '*salilam*' (water) in the Vedic text for *kārana* seems to have given the clue to the pictorial representation of *kārana* as all-pervading water in the mythological version. The One with Its power *Swadhā* has appeared as *Nārāyana* with His *Yogamāyā*.

From the mythological version the following truths announced by the Vedas regarding *Pralaya* and *Srishti* are imprinted on one's mind: God with His power *Māyā* alone existed during *Pralaya*,

[1] *Rg. Vd.* X. 129. 1–3

everything else lay reduced to the causal state typified by all-pervading water; on the eve of Creation by His will and through His *Māyā* was projected *Brahmā* (*Hiranyagarbha*) out of Him and through *Brahmā* the rest of Creation. A little interpretation of the mythological picture will yield these Vedic truths about *Pralaya* and *Srishti*. Of course, very crude minds may not go so far as to grasp the underlying idea; yet through the picture they are sure to get the minimum truth, and that is of no mean value, namely, that God with His holy consort (*Shakti*) is the sole source of Creation. He is both its efficient and material cause.

In this way the pictorial representations of mythology stamp on the mass mind the fundamentals of Hindu faith regarding God, nature and soul.

Mythology, moreover, has furnished the Hindu society with countless inspiring ideals culled from history, tradition and legends. Hundreds of shining characters have in this way been burnt into the mass mind of Hindu India. They are still regarded as model patterns of Hindu life to be emulated by all and sundry. Thus the king, the hero, the householder, the hermit, the devotee, the father, the mother, the wife, the husband, the son, the brother, the servant—each of these and of many more has at least one blazing *Paurānika* (mythological) character as an age-old model. Rāma, Krishna, Arjuna, Yudhishthira, Bhishma, Vasishtha, Vidura, Nala,

Harishchandra, Karna, Gāndhāri, Sitā, Sāvitri, Lakshmana, Bharata and Mahāvira may be mentioned among the numerous ideals that live to this day as perennial sources of spiritual inspiration for moulding Hindu life and conduct on correct lines.

Then the stories themselves are mines of wisdom. Each inscribes on the heart an important lesson. It usually illustrates a theme that has a direct bearing on some aspect of the ideal Hindu life and conduct. The lesson may be on one or other spiritual law, or on some course of religious practice or on some ethical principle, or on the specific duties (*dharma*) of an individual according to his stage of life, as well as social status and relationship.

Righteousness is sure to triumph in the end; greed, lust, jealousy, pride and all that evil brood cannot hold out for long and must go down in the end. This spiritual law ('*Yato dharmastato jayah*') is engraved on one's mind by most of the stories. This particular lesson, which is almost the burden of every mythological song or saga of the Hindus, has gone deep into the Hindu mind and coloured its entire outlook on life. Through it the Hindu mind has been trained to rely more on the Spirit than on brute force. The might of the warrior must be backed up by right living and right conduct; he must always take up arms for a righteous cause; else his fate is sealed in spite of his extraordinary military prowess. The fall of Rāvana, monstrous superman with evil propensities depicted in the *Rāmāyana*, as well as the fall of the Kauravas, the champions of unworthy desires, in spite of the numerical strength and outstanding leadership of their army described in the *Mahābhārata*, drives this lesson home to the Hindu mind.

Then again, the presence of Rāma and Krishna as Divine Incarnations in these two legends respectively has imparted a spiritual value to all their contents. Meditation on the life-story of an *Avatāra* being a spiritual practice of immense value, both the *Rāmāyana* and the *Mahābhārata* offer ample facilities and inspiration for such practice. Through these legends God as Rāma or Krishna appears to have come to our very door; we almost see them and touch the hem of their garments. *Shrimad Bhāgavatam*, containing among other things an impressive picture of another portion of the life-story of Sri Krishna, has also a similar effect on the Hindu mind.

Another highly interesting and instructive feature of the mythological stories is that through them one gets wonderful solutions of puzzling situations arising out of an apparent conflict of duties. Rāma's duty towards his wife is outweighed by his duty towards his subjects; Bharata's duty towards his ambitious and jealous mother is superseded by that towards his righteous brother; Vibhishana's duty towards his lustful brother is cancelled by that towards their righteous Divine foe; Karna's duty towards his son yields place to that towards his hungry guest. Through hundreds of such episodes the Hindus have been given practical guidance with regard to the choice of duties in embarrassing situations. In every case the individual is directed to rise above the demands of the flesh and of narrow selfishness and soar towards the Spirit. This seems to be the working formula for solving any conflict of duties.

Besides painting in brilliant colours the cardinal virtues through countless tales, the mythological literature of the Hindus contains brilliant and lucid discourses on philosophy and practical religion interspersed between the main narratives. A dramatic setting together with a lucid style makes these discourses interesting, easy and impressive. That is why it is from these that the bulk of the Hindus take their lessons on religion and philosophy. The *Gitā* and the *Chandi*, easily the most popular of the Hindu *Shāstras* of this day, are such interludes of discourses on such dramatic settings within the main narrative of the *Māhābhārata* and the *Mārkandeya Purāna* respectively.

Thus mythology, through its pictorial representation of the highly subtle and abstract teachings of the Vedas, its impressive character-painting, instructive stories and illuminating discourses, goes a long way to spiritualize the Hindu outlook on life.

XXI

THE HINDU OUTLOOK ON LIFE

THE contents of Hindu faith regarding God, nature and soul have come down to us through the *Shāstras* from the days of the *Rig-Veda*. Since then, through thousands of years, they have been amplified and elucidated by the later *Shāstras* and verified by the realization of the seers of every age including our own. The findings of the Hindu *rishis* (seers) reveal certain unalterable, eternal truths about life and existence, such as the immanence of God in nature and the divinity of the soul. These may be said to be the fundamentals of the Hindu faith, which for this reason, is also called the Eternal Religion (*sanātana dharma*).

It is on such eternal verities that the entire structure of Hindu life is built. And this is perhaps why this structure has lasted through scores of centuries. Even invasion, colonization and domination by various alien races have not affected the general tenor of Hindu life to any appreciable extent. Unlike the Assyrians, Babylonians, Egyptians, Greeks and Romans, the Hindus of this day have not changed from their ancient forefathers beyond recognition. The *mantras* even of the hoary *Rig-Veda* are still recited by them, and their conduct even now is regulated by the *Shāstras* as in the days of old.

This is not because the Hindus, in their ignorance, are foolishly sticking to a phase of medievalism, as some moderners would have us believe. The reason is to be sought elsewhere. The Hindus cannot forsake what is eternally true. It is on the rocky foundation of such truths that their society is built. This structure is bound to collapse and become extinct if it be uprooted from such foundation. But that is not to be.

As centuries rolled by, the superstructure of Hindu life, no doubt, suffered wear and tear. But before it could give way, an *Avatāra* or an *Achārya* appeared in time to give it a fresh lease of life by repairing and remodelling it according to the demand of changed circumstances. Thus it has been going on through the ages, and all the while its foundation on the rock of spiritual truths has remained the same. The *Shruti* (the Vedas) has persisted throughout the ages as the supreme authority. As the repository of the eternal truths discovered by the *rishis*, it has all along been holding its sway over all other *Shāstras*. These others, that is, the *Smritis*, have been modified from time to time by outstanding spiritual personages to suit the changing environments of the Hindu society. But this has been done without deviating from the fundamentals of the Hindu faith as revealed through the *Shruti*.

Such a process has been at work since the birth

of Hinduism. Rigidity with regard to the fundamentals and elasticity in readjusting the externals have been the technique through which the Hindus have succeeded in living through millenniums.

The essential divinity of man, as we have said, is one of the fundamentals of Hindu faith. His soul being none other than God, man has always within him the potentiality of becoming divine in all his bearings. He can never be damned for ever for any act of his, however outrageous that may be. Sins are no more than mistakes committed through ignorance. For such sins one has, of course, to pay by suffering pain here or hereafter. However, he grows wiser through such sufferings and proceeds through repeated births till the Divinity within him is completely manifested. Everyone is to reach this blessed goal. Sinners, therefore, are not to be condemned. They should be treated with sympathy and helped out of ignorance.

The fact is, as long as man does not realize his oneness with the Universal Spirit and remains attached to his physical body and the physical universe, he continues in a state of bondage. He is almost a brute in human form. Yet Hinduism does not damn him for ever. It helps him onward step by step till the brute in him disappears altogether yielding place to God.

To speed up this glorious transformation is, according to Hinduism, the very object of human life. Everything else is considered as a means to this end. Scholarship, wealth, progeny have only secondary values in so far as they contribute towards the advancement of spiritual life. If they cannot be made to serve this main purpose, they are trash. Anything done at the cost of spiritual life only goes to retard one's progress towards perfection.

However, so long as man remains tied to his flesh and hankers after sense-objects, he is a poor little creature buffeted helplessly by every turn of fortune. He is not aware of the glory of his real Self. He hugs Its shadow as his self. Identifying himself with the physical body and sense-organs, man appears during this stage to be a bond-slave of passions. Swayed by anger, malice, lust and conceit and, above all, by selfishness, he makes a miserable show of what he really is. His Divine Soul is clouded by his turbid mind. What he claims to be his self is a very crude, narrow, low and perverted image of his real Self.

This is the apparent lower self of man that keeps him bound to the plane of desires and whirls him through repeated births in this world and the next. This is the bird on the tree eating savoury fruits; this is the entity described as darkness.[1] Through suitable spiritual practice this apparent lower self, however, disappears in course of time, releasing man for ever from the grip of the sense-objects and

[1] See *supra* Chap. XIX.

sense-organs and installing him in the domain of eternal peace within.

Spiritual practice consists essentially in battering this bastion of ignorance, this lower self, till it is reduced to nothingness. This is done by rejecting its demands in the shape of ever changing and ever renewing desires. Renunciation of desires is, therefore, the fundamental requisite of spiritual practice. It is the very breath of spiritual life. Through it alone Immortality can be attained, the Divinity in man can be manifested. There is absolutely no other way. Complete renunciation is the ideal; through it alone man can realize his oneness with God. Of course, this cannot be accomplished in a day, nor by all at the same time. It is the ideal, no doubt, but it has to be reached through stages, each man starting from where he stands. The senses and the mind have to be broken gradually. This is why the *Pravritti Mārga* sanctions even the pursuit of desires within certain limits.

However, the goal of perfection may be reached only through absolute renunciation of desires. One has to gain perfect control over nature, external and internal, when the Divine Soul within manifests Itself completely. And this may be done either by psychic control (*Rāja-yoga*), or philosophy (*Jnāna-yoga*), or worship (*Bhakti-yoga*), or work (*Karma-yoga*), or by any combination of these. This indeed, is the whole of religion. Hindu *dharma* with all its temples, images, rituals and mythologies, with all its varying shades of spiritual ideologies, points unmistakably to this.

Thus religion with the Hindus is an immensely practical affair. It is intended to govern one's entire life. It is to regulate a man's life and conduct in such a way as may enable him to advance as far as possible towards Divinity from where he starts. The practical courses of religion must, therefore, fit in with his natural requirements, depending on the stage of his spiritual development. These must conform to his taste, capacity and temperament. Each man has to take up the course that suits him best. This is called *adhikārivāda*, that is, the doctrine of 'each according to his capacity'.

Another important fact announced by the Hindu *Shāstras* in this connection is that the spiritual progress made during one life is not lost. The stage reached by a man in one life becomes the starting-point of the next. Nothing can undo what has been achieved. Evil deeds bring in sufferings and are thus expiated; they may for a while, moreover, cloud one's spiritual vision and suppress the urge for spiritual growth, but they cannot permanently undo what has been achieved by spiritual practice. Virtue and vice, according to Hinduism, do not cancel each other; each brings its own results separately. And one rises above both on the dawning of Self-knowledge.

The immanence of God in nature is another outstanding spiritual truth admitted by all schools of Hindu thought. Beneath the ever changing diversities on the face of nature, there is an underlying unity in God. He runs through all like the thread through the pearls of a necklace.[1] *Ishwara* (God) manifests Himself as the ceaseless and countless objects in nature, and by governing them all from within as *Antaryāmi* He produces the matchless symphony of nature.

Unity in diversity, therefore, is regarded by the Hindus as the fundamental law of nature. They are taught to appreciate the need and function of both these factors, unity as well as diversity, in creating the symphony of nature. Diversity is no accident. It has a meaning and a value. It proceeds from the urge for Divine manifestation. "I am one—may I be many"—this omnipotent will of the Lord fulfils itself by projecting infinite diversities. His *Prakriti* (Cosmic Energy) has the potentiality of throwing out endlessly new forms. This is why nature bears on it the stamp of manifoldness. Even on the same tree no two leaves are found to be exactly alike.

Indeed, it is the diversity on the surface projected and controlled by the Divine Unity inside that gives rise to the beauty, order and harmony of nature. Those who are conscious of the inner

[1] Cf. *Gitā* VII. 7.

unity enjoy this beauty more than anybody else. Love for all and 'purest joy serene' well up from their soul, cover the whole world and transform it verily into a kingdom of heaven.

Hinduism teaches us to take a leaf out of nature. We are advised to stick to this principle of unity in diversity while dealing with all human problems, individual and social, related to all spheres of our activity and interest. In all these we should do well to accommodate as many diversities as possible without overlooking the underlying unity. In this way, we should imitate the Divine pattern in nature, instead of seeking a dull, mechanical and monotonous uniformity. Harmony, and not rigid uniformity, is the Divine law of nature.

Each soul is potentially divine. The difference between man and man lies just on the surface. There is everlasting Divine Unity at the core. We are born on the surface, in nature. We have to dive below nature and become free by reaching the core of the Universal Spirit (*Paramātman*). This is the game, and we have to play it out. This is the *lilā* (sport) of the Lord. The game will be over as soon as we reach the Great One.

Hence, in our relations with fellow-men, anything that makes for unity is good for our spiritual progress. Selfless love makes for unity; therefore it is good for us. This is why we are asked to culture such love through the selfless service of our fellow-men. It is sure to help us on towards the goal of Divine Unity. We have to expand our hearts through such service till we succeed in embracing the entire world as our very self. Indeed, expansion of heart is the rhythm of spiritual life.

The Hindus are taught to expand their hearts through renunciation and service. This is their *dharma* (religion). In the scheme of Hindu life this *dharma* of selfless service is a prominent factor. It is the very corner-stone of their social structure. As it helps one to rise above one's crude lower self, it is prescribed for all as a potent purifier of the mind. Hindu life is supposed to be a continued performance of such *dharma* in the shape of one's prescribed duties (*swadharma*).

The relation between individuals is expressed in terms of duties and not of rights. The assertion of rights and consequent scramble for power and privilege very often proceed from lust, conceit and crass selfishness. Hence it has the risk of degrading man spiritually. This is why, though the Hindus are exhorted by their *Shāstras* to stand up for a really righteous cause, they are made conscious more of their duties than of their rights. For it is through the discharge of the prescribed duties that one may expand one's heart and advance spiritually. Hence these duties of any individual are said to be his *dharma*. Thus the parents and their children, the husband and the wife, the king and his subjects are mutually related through their respective *dharma* (duties). Then again, each individual has his own code of duties called his *swadharma*, according to his stage of life (*āshrama*) and station in society (*varna*). Each of these duties requires one to serve others, forgoing the intensely selfish demands of the lower self. Thus through renunciation and service every Hindu is required to expand his heart and advance steadily towards the goal of perfection. And when one, renouncing all desires, performs one's duties purely as a worship of the Lord, one reaches the goal quickly.[1] Thus the entire range of Hindu life, from the crudest stage right up to the highest, is a graded course of renunciation and service that gradually lifts one up to the great vision of the central Divine Unity in the midst of all diversities.

Hatred, jealousy, selfishness and all that emphasize the difference between man and man and give rise to discord and disunion lie at the opposite pole. They proceed from a narrow self-centred outlook on life, representing what may be called a contraction of the heart. When man, in his ignorance about his really divine nature, foolishly idolizes his lower self, his heart suffers such contraction. This acts like poison on one's spiritual life and should, therefore, be shunned by all means. This is why lust, anger, greed, infatuation, conceit

[1] Cf. *Gita* XVIII. 46.

and jealousy are reckoned as foes (*ripu*) by the Hindus.

Among the many and diverse, one should ceaselessly and consistently strive to see the Eternal One. This is verily the key-note of Hindu life. It was precisely this attitude that gave rise to the distinctive features of the Hindu culture. And it was this that breathed a vigorous life into the Hindu society of old, enabling it to embrace the people of many alien races and creeds within its outstretched arms. Neither with sword nor with fire did the ancient Hindus spread their culture. Universal love born of purity and God-vision was their only weapon. It was this vision of unity in diversity that gave them the strength to expand their fold by elevating culturally the aborigines of this land, and later the Bactrian Greeks, the Hunas, the Sakas, as also the different peoples of distant lands in southeast Asia. Indeed, this vision enabled Hinduism to make its healthy cultural influence felt practically by the whole of Asia, and maybe by Greece, too, the cradle of Western civilization.

The process of expansion was simple. The vision of the underlying unity endowed the ancient Hindus with a wonderful breadth of outlook that enabled them to love the people of diverse stocks, mix with them and raise their life and thoughts to a higher level. It was impossible for them to think of exterminating the aliens or of destroying their cultural heritages. Was not each group a type manifested by God Himself? Was it not a sacred thing? Was not its cultural heritage a kind of organic growth representing just a particular variety of human culture evolved through centuries? The ancient Hindus had the wisdom of appreciating the sanctity and worth of each group of aliens and its cultural heritage, however crude that might be.

This was why the Hindus accepted all these as they stood, and only gave them an upward turn by a very gentle touch. They only breathed the spirit of Hinduism into these various groups and made a place for them within the Hindu fold. Their religious practices and social customs were only tuned to the fundamentals of the Hindu faith and then ushered bodily into Hinduism. It was in this way that diverse religious practices and codes of living found their way into Hindu religion and made it, in course of time, almost an epitome of all religions. Hinduism in those days had the power to assimilate foreign elements and expand. This, surely, is a sign of life. Indeed, the Hindus remained vigorously alive as long as their vision of unity in diversity was not blurred.

Whenever this vision became dim, the Hindus sank into torpor, and their dynamic religion became almost moribund. Losing sight of the underlying Divine Unity, the Hindus during such periods of spiritual inanition would become narrow, bigoted and sectarian in their outlook and stoop to emphasize division and subdivisions of their own society and to ostracize all foreigners. Scramble for power and privilege would ensue, giving rise to hatred and malice. Losing their grip on the fundamental requisites of spiritual progress, namely, renunciation and service, they would become engrossed merely with the externals of religion. Thus straying farther and farther away from the ancient ideas and ideals, they would, during such periods, make a mess of the lofty and catholic religion.

Happily such periods would not come to stay. They would invariably be followed by a rising tide of spirituality. We are facing such a phenomenon today. An ebb-tide of our cultural life is just over, a resurgence is in the offing. The Hindus, after a period of torpor, are becoming conscious over again of the precious fundamentals of their faith. And very naturally, Hinduism has already begun to show unmistakable signs of its original dynamism.

The Hindus of this day are hearkening back to the life-giving messages of the Upanishads. Above the din and clamour of sectarian and communal feuds of centuries is rising in ever growing volume and intensity the clarion call of the ancient *rishis*: "Whatever exists in this transient world has to be pervaded by the Lord (through one's contemplation). Enjoy them all through renunciation (of the

lower self). Don't covet any body else's property."[1]
The same Lord has to be seen in all and through
all. Thus the Hindus are being revitalized to work
out their age-old precept of seeking harmony in
everything about them through the vision of unity
in diversity. They are becoming inspired to appreciate the worth and beauty of diversities in
every sphere of human interest.

In the field of religion, variety is being looked
upon as a source of richness of human culture. Just
as one coat cannot fit everybody, so also one religion
cannot suit everyone. As a family has to provide
each of its members with a separate suit of clothes
according to its requirement, so also the great
human family has to provide its various groups with
distinct religions suited to their distinct tastes and
capacities. Diversity of taste and capacity has to be
accepted as an ineffaceable fact of nature and has
to be provided for. And this has actually been done
through the introduction of the various religions.
They have no reason to quarrel with one another
for supremacy. Each is a correct path to the same
goal of perfection; and each has its use for a
particular group of human beings. This has been
taught, time and again, by the Hindu saints and
seers. After a lapse, the Hindus are again becoming
aware of this fact in the light of Sri Rāmakrishna's
life and teachings. They are fast becoming con-

[1] *Ish. Up.* I.

vinced that each group should stick to its own religion and, at the same time, maintain a reverent attitude towards all others as so many diverse paths discovered through the ages for arriving at the same goal. The vision of unity in diversity in this sphere is sure to give a quietus to all communal and sectarian squabbles.

The same vision in the social sphere is bound to work miracles. It will rejuvenate the Hindu society and enable it to contribute substantially towards the spiritual progress of mankind. The unworthy fight for power and privilege has to be given up. The age-old scheme of life characterized by renunciation and service has to be revived. Consciousness of duty has again to gain prominence over that of right. The relations between individuals and groups within the society have to be readjusted accordingly. Every individual, be he a son or a servant, is a manifestation of God, and as such he has to be treated with due regard. There may exist diversity of castes, but there must not be any hatred or rancour between them. Each group is sacred. Each has its place and function. Each has its part to play in the symphony of Hindu life. It has, therefore, to be treated with proper regard. None should be kept down. Each group must have a scope for cultural uplift. Things like untouchability have to be banned for ever. Signs are not lacking to show that the Hindus of the present day are becoming alive to the need of overhauling their society in this way in the light of the fundamentals of their faith.

This time they may not stop merely at this. Revitalized by such overhauling, they are expected to extend their vision of unity in diversity beyond the framework of their society. It seems that their *dharma* of selfless service is going to be extended to all corners of the earth. The races, nations and all that, may be diverse. So also may be the structures of their social, political and economic life. Such varieties related to human groups certainly add to the beauty and richness of the entire human society. Through each God is manifesting Himself. Each represents a type projected by Him. Each is holy. Each has a mission to fulfil. Each has to contribute something substantial towards the growth of mankind. This fundamental fact of Divine Unity underlying all human varieties preached by the Hindu *Shāstras* is not going to be ignored any longer.

None should be hated, none should be oppressed or injured in any way. We have to help them all, if we can, by removing the obstacles from their way. Such selfless service of all in the social, economic, political and spiritual fields, without making any distinction between castes, creeds, races or nations, is required of us by our religion. This is our *dharma*. Instead of keeping it confined within the limits of our own society, we have to extend its practice all over the world. The words '*mlechchha*' and '*yavana*' betraying hatred and arrogance are not in tune with the spirit of Hinduism. They must have been coined during some period of spiritual decadence. These words bespeak crudities unworthy of the Hindus, whose ideal is to see all in the Self and the Self in all. The Hindus in the near future are expected to ban these words for ever and to regard every human individual as *Nārāyana* (the Lord). Inspired by the lofty message of their age-old Upanishads, the Hindus have the potency of making, through the selfless service of all, the diverse races on earth aware of their underlying Divine Unity and thus of producing an unprecedented symphony all over the world. This, perhaps, is the mission for fulfilling which the Hindus are still living.

BEARING OF HINDUISM ON INTERNATIONAL PEACE

TEACHINGS

Hinduism does hold that there may be occasions for righteous war. So long as human nature is not radically transformed, evil-doers will have to be quelled for the peace and security of human society, and these necessary efforts may at times assume the proportions of even world-wars. A radical transformation of the entire human society is something which the Hindus never expect.

Hinduism holds that a soldier fighting for a righteous cause is performing a meritorious act. Moreover, this religion maintains that man can rise to such a stage of spiritual perfection that he can kill people without being touched in the least by sin.

Yet, Hinduism has ideas and ideals that tend primarily to put an end to strifes and discords.

Nature appears to work out her plan of warring varieties even on the human plane. In external nature there seems to be a perpetual process of forging varieties, and in internal nature there is the incessant claim of the ego for superiority, special esteem and privilege on behalf of each variety. Conflicts between individuals as well as between groups become inevitable. Nothing less than faith in the Unity behind nature and a corresponding readjustment of internal nature can be expected to minimize these conflicts.

Hinduism emphasizes the truth of Unity behind the apparent diversities of nature. Nature, consisting both of matter and mind, is only an appearance; the only Reality is God. The real self of man is no other than God, his mind and body are mere forms.

Man suffers and makes others suffer only because, obscured by primal ignorance, he does not recognize his real self and identifies himself with his body and mind, which are mere forms. Hinduism asks man precisely to get rid of this ignorance and realize his essential unity with the rest of creation. This state is what the Hindus call *Moksha* or liberation from the bonds of nature, and this, in their eyes, is the goal of human life.

In order to attain this goal, one is required to take his stand on the truth of his unity with all and train his mind not to emphasize the superficial diversities of nature. He is required to look upon all as manifestations of God, and love and serve all without any distinction of caste, creed or colour, even as he loves and serves himself.

Thus the path of self-sacrifice and service has been chalked out by Hinduism for every individual. This will work out his own perfection by manifesting his Divine Self and certainly contribute towards the peace and well-being of society. For the sake of being freed from the bonds of nature, for attaining eternal peace and blessedness, the individual has to love and serve others, trying all the while to feel his essential unity in God with all that exist.

Struggle and fight for selfish ends may be a necessity for the evolution of brute life; but the path of human progress right up to the eminence of a Buddha or Jesus lies through renunciation and service. Conscious practice of these can completely reverse the egocentric nature of man and make him perfectly immune from all impulses of envy and hatred. The ideal man, according to Hinduism, is he who sees 'the self in all and all in the self'.

If such a programme for individual life could be adopted on a worldwide scale, universal peace would become a settled fact in a short time. But we consider that to be an empty dream. Mankind cannot be expected to change its nature by a miracle. A few will, of course, struggle for spiritual growth and try to live up to high ideals, but the majority is sure to tread the rut-bound path of self-aggrandizement, fight, coercion and competition. Yet, if within all groups of the human society vigorous efforts be made even by minorities to realize the living Unity behind nature through love and selfless service, something substantial may be attained towards minimizing discords between the different groups.

In the history of Hindu civilization we find several epochs when by the intense efforts of saints and seers these lofty ideals of selflessness and service were made very prominent both in individual and collective life. During these epochs the entire Hindu society gave wonderful demonstrations of concord, harmony, liberality and tolerance. The original Hindu programme of life in all spheres as a graded course of renunciation and service for manifesting the divinity in man would get a fresh lease and sanction during these periods, and the group-mind also would give evidence of a fresh inspiration and broadening of outlook.

ATTITUDE TOWARDS OTHERS

This explains how the Hindus could receive with open arms the persecuted and refugees of other religions and other nations. The persecuted Israelites and Zoroastrians did find a peaceful shelter on the soil of the Hindus. In its attitude towards other religions, Hinduism has all along been tolerant to a degree. The Hindus believe that all religions lead alike to the same goal, namely, God, the only Reality, who appears through different names and different forms to different devotees.

PRAYERS

In the Hindu scriptures one finds abundant mention of the truth of One Existence, and the necessity of realization of the same for individual salvation. Prayers for universal peace and well-being, though not quite so profusely mentioned, have found a place in the Hindu scriptures. A few extracts rendered into English will show the universal character of these prayers:

"May all be happy. May all be free from disease. May all realize what is good. May none be subject to misery."

"May the wicked become virtuous. May the virtuous attain tranquillity. May the tranquil be free from bonds. May the freed make others free."

"May all be free from dangers. May all realize what is good. May all be actuated by noble thoughts. May all rejoice everywhere."

"May good betide all peoples. May the sovereigns rule the earth following the righteous path. May all beings attain to their welfare. May all the world be prosperous and happy."

During the glorious epochs of spiritual revival the chords of the Hindu heart would be made to emit such a sweet note of universal peace and harmony.

But each of these periods of spiritual revival was closely followed by a period of decadence. Owing to the natural gravitation of man towards selfishness and superficialities, the real spirit of religion has at times been almost buried under meaningless non-essentials. People would lose sight of the central truths, misunderstand and misinterpret the sacred texts and foolishly allow even grossly unspiritual elements to masquerade in the name of religion.

OUR ORGANIZATION WORKING IN A WAY FOR UNIVERSAL PEACE

Hindu society had been passing through such a phase of decadence, when the life and teachings of Sri Rāmakrishna (1836–1886) resuscitated the spirit of Religion, and society has since been showing sure signs of rising from its temporary torpor.

The lofty ideas and ideals of Hinduism have once again become clear in the light of Sri Rāmakrishna's wonderful realization of spiritual truths, and it is to preach and practise these that this Rāmakrishna Order of monks has been established. We believe that the ideas and ideals of our religion will again be the moving forces of the Hindu society, purge it to a considerable extent of the impurities accumulated during a couple of centuries, and contribute towards invoking universal peace and harmony, for which such a keen anxiety is being felt all round the world.

Our organization is dedicated to working towards this glorious end, in its humble way, through humanitarian service and preaching of the message of the grand living Unity behind the apparent diversities on the surface of creation.

If, through all the groups of mankind, vigorous efforts are made to emphasize the underlying unity more than the apparent multiplicity of nature, and also to urge individual as well as collective life to tread the path of sacrifice and service as the only path of human progress, we believe that some anxiety at least over the future of the human race may be set at rest, and our race may advance a step forward towards all-round peace and happiness. An era of universal peace and well-being, of universal brotherhood of man, may be a dream, and this dream may perhaps never be realized. But it can never be denied that concerted efforts for realizing such a dream, for bringing about concord and .harmony, will go to reduce human sufferings to their minimum; and this itself is quite a significant achievement, for which the best efforts of all lovers of humanity should by all means be concentrated.

[*Paper sent to an International Peace Conference in 1932*]

GLOSSARY†

áchamana Sipping water from the palm of the hand, a preliminary simple rite connected with ritualistic worship;
  (rinsing the mouth).
achara Incapable of moving about.
áchára Conduct; (usage; custom).
Áchárya Spiritual teacher; propounder of a doctrine; an exalted spiritual personage born with the mission of propagat-
  ing spiritual truths.
Adharma Irreligion; unrighteousness.
adhikári-váda The doctrine upholding the necessity of prescribing a distinct course of discipline for each spiritual aspirant
  according to his capacity.
adhishthátri devatá Presiding deity.
adhyása A Vedántic word for the illusion of seeing one thing
  as another.
Áditya A Hindu deity.
adrishta (*Lit.*, unseen) Fate; luck.
Advaita-váda The doctrine of Non-dualism (of the Vedánta
  school teaching the absolute oneness of God, soul and
  universe).
Ágama A class of *Tántrika* literature. *See* Tantra(s).
agni: Agni* Fire. *See* bhuta(s): *A Hindu deity.
ahamkára Ego.
aishwarya Spiritual power; (wealth).
ajnána: Ajnána* Ignorance: *Primal Ignorance. *See* Avidyá.
ákásha Earth, *See* bhuta(s).
ákásha-váni Ethereal voice, heavenly voice.
Ákhyána Narrative; a variety of mythological narrative.
ambara Sky; ether; cloth; garment.
anádi Without any beginning.
anáhata dhwani A highly subtle, spontaneous perpetual sound
  audible to one in a state of deep concentration of mind.
ánandamaya kosha The sheath of bliss. *See* kosha(s).

† This glossary of Sanskrit words gives principally the senses in
which they have been used in this book.

Ananta Nāga Name of a mythical hydra-headed serpent (also called *Shesha* and *Vāsuki*).

annamaya kosha The gross sheath (made of food), *i.e.*, the physical body. *See* kosha(s).

antahkarana (*Lit.*, the inner instrument) The mind and the subtle sense-organs.

Antaryāmi (*Lit.*, one who controls from within) God is so called because He resides in everything and controls it from within.

antarjyoti (*Lit.*, having an effulgent interior) Self-effulgent.

ap Water. *See* bhuta(s).

Apara(ā) Lower; inferior.

Aparabrahman *See* Hiranyagarbha.

Aparā Prakriti The Lower Cosmic Energy, through which God projects all forms in nature, gross and fine.

ārātrika (ārati) Waving lights etc. before an image or symbol, a rite connected with ritualistic worship.

Ārya(s) Indo-Aryans.

Ārya dharma Religion of the Indo-Aryans, *i.e.*, the Vedic Religion.

Āryāvarta The tract in northern India occupied by the Indo-Aryans in the early stage of their expansion.

āsana Sitting posture related to the practice of concentration. *See* Ashtānga-yoga.

āshrama Any of the four stages of life of a Hindu, *viz.*, *Brahmacharya, Gārhasthya, Vānaprastha* and *Sannyāsa*.

Ashtānga-yoga (*Lit.*, *yoga* consisting of eight limbs or parts) *Rāja-yoga* is so called as it prescribes eight successive courses of spiritual discipline, *viz.*, *yama, niyama, āsana, prānāyāma, pratyāhāra, dhāranā, dhyāna* and *samādhi*.

ashubha Evil.

Ashwamedha yajna Horse-sacrifice,—an elaborate Vedic ceremonial.

ashwattha Peepul tree.

atindriya Beyond the reach of the senses.

Ātma-jnāna Self-knowledge.

Ātman The Self; Soul.

ātyantika Pralaya Absolute Dissolution (when the universe together with its root-cause, Primal Nescience, disappears completely) on attainment of complete Self-knowledge.

āvarani shakti One of the aspects or component powers of Nescience functioning as the veiler of Reality.

Avatāra Incarnation of God (*i.e.*, a descent of the Universal Spirit).

Avidyā Primal Ignorance, the Divine Power of Nescience (through which the Absolute appears as the cosmos according to the Non-dualistic Vedānta school).

avyakta: Avyakta* Unmanifested: *Cosmic Energy in the potential condition (as it remains during the state of Dissolution): the Divine Power of Nescience; same as Avidyā and Māyā.

Āyurveda The science of Medicine including Surgery.

baddha In a state of bondage.

bandhana Bondage.

Bauddha Buddhist; Buddhistic.

Bhagavān The Lord (*Lit.*, one endowed with the six attributes, *viz.*, infinite spiritual power, righteousness, glory, splendour, knowledge and renunciation).

bhakta Devotee; a follower of the Path of Love.

bhakti Devotion; intense love for God.

Bhakti-yoga The Path of Love—one of the four fundamental types of spiritual discipline.

Bhakti-yogi One going through the scheduled spiritual discipline of the Path of Love.

bhautika Made of *bhutas*. See bhuta(s).

bhāva Attitude mostly expressing a particular relationship with God; any of the five such attitudes prescribed by Vaishnavism, *viz.*, *shānta*, *dāsya*, *sakhya*, *vātsalya* and *madhura* (also, emotion; ecstasy; existence; entity).

bhoga Experience; perception; enjoyment.

bhogabhumi Land of experience.

bhogya Object of experience.

bhoktā Subject of experience.

bhuta(s) (*Lit.*, what has come into being, an entity as opposed to the unmanifested) Any of the five elementary constituents of the universe, *viz.*, *ākāsha*, *vāyu*, *agni* (*tejas*), *ap* and *kshiti* (called *sukshma bhutas*, *mahā-bhutas* or *tanmātras*), —according to Hindu cosmogony, these are the earliest and subtlest manifestations of the Absolute, as such they compose whatever exists on the subtle (mental) plane; after being compounded with one another in a particular way (*see* panchikarana) they become gross *bhutas* and serve as units in the make-up of the physical universe; also, a living being.

bhuta-shuddhi A ritualistic process connected with *Tāntrika* worship.

Bhuta-yajna An offering to subhuman creatures,—one of the five sacrificial rites enjoined on all householders.

Bhuvaneshwari Name of God as the Divine Mother in a particular form.

Brahma(n) (*Lit.*, the Great One) Impersonal God; the Absolute Reality.

Brahmā God as the Creator,—one of the Hindu Trinity, the other two being *Vishnu*, the Preserver and *Shiva*, the Destroyer; also, the first of the created beings, *Hiranyagarbha*, the Cosmic Intelligence—a Hindu deity.

Brahma-vidyā Knowledge about the Ultimate Reality.

Brahmacharya The first stage of Hindu life, *viz.*, celibate student's stage. *See* āshrama.

Brahmaloka The highest world (presided over by *Hiranyagarbha, i.e., Brahmā*).

Brāhmana(s) A section of each of the Vedas dwelling on the meaning and use of the Vedic hymns; a primary social group. *See* varna.

Brahmānda The universe; nature comprehending all entities, gross and fine.

buddhi Intellect, intelligence, a function of the mind; the first and the most prominent component of the subtle body,—with which, according to Non-dualistic Vedānta philosophy, the real Self appears to be identified giving rise to the illusory appearance of the individual soul, the subject of action and experience.

chaitanya Consciousness.

Chaitanyamayi All-Consciousness,—an attribute of the Divine Mother.

chakshu Eye; the subtle organs of sight corresponding to the eyes. *See* indriya(s).

Chandi Name of God as the Divine Mother in a particular form; also, one of the very popular scriptural texts.

chara Capable of moving about.

Chārvāka The founder of a materialistic school of philosophy; pertaining to this school of thought.

chitta-shuddhi   Purification of the mind.

daiva vāni   Heavenly voice (actually heard by pure souls).

Darshana(s)   Any system of Hindu philosophy.

dāsya   The attitude of a devotee expressing the relationship of a servant with God. *See* bhāva.

deva   A deity; the highest order of superhuman beings; one belonging to this order.

Devaloka   One of the higher worlds; the world of the deities.

Deva-yajna   One of the five sacrificial rites enjoined on all householders, in which oblations are offered to various deities.

devatā   A god or goddess; a deity.

dhāranā   Repeated attempt at fixing the mind on a single object. *See* Ashtānga-yoga.

dharma   (*Lit.*, that which holds up the existence of a thing) Essential quality; religion; code of duties; duty.

dhyāna   Meditation; the state of uninterrupted concentration of the mind on a single object. *See* Ashtānga-yoga.

dikshā   Initiation (into any form of spiritual discipline).

dikshita   Initiated (into any form of spiritual discipline).

divyāchāra   (*Lit.*, conduct of the godly ones) A *Tāntrika* course of spiritual discipline meant for the pure and advanced aspirants.

Durgā   Name of God as the Divine Mother in a particular form.

Dvaita-vāda   Doctrine of Dualism.

ekārnava   One boundless sea in which state the universe is described figuratively to exist during Dissolution (the potential cause of the next creation being described as the waters, *kārana-salila*, of this all-pervading sea).

Ganapati   (Ganesha) A Hindu deity; God in a particular form as the chosen Ideal of a Hindu sect.

Gānapatya   A Hindu sect worshipping God as Ganapati; a member of this sect; pertaining to this sect.

gandha   Smell; the sensation of smell.

Gārhasthya   The second stage of Hindu life, *viz.*, the married householder's stage. *See* āshrama.

gauna(i)   Secondary; indirect.

gauni bhakti   Culture of devotion through rituals as a preliminary course on the Path of Love. *See* bhakti.

guna   Property; trait; aspect.

guru   Spiritual guide.

Hiranyagarbha   Cosmic Intelligence, a Hindu deity, the highest created being through whom God projects the physical universe. Also called *Brahmā, Prāna, Sutrātmā, Apara-brahman* and *Mahat Brahman*.

homa   Usually a concluding rite of *Tāntrika* worship consisting of oblations to a sacred fire,—a survival of the Vedic sacrifical rites.

hridaya   Heart.

Indra   A Hindu deity.

indriya(s)   Subtle sense-organs in the psychic (subtle) body corresponding to the grosser instruments of knowledge and action on the physical body like the eyes, ears, hands, feet, etc.

Ishta   (*Lit.*, an object of desire) The chosen Ideal,—the particular Divine Form through which a spiritual aspirant contemplates on God; also, sacrificial rite.

Ishta-nishthā   Unflinching devotion to one's chosen Ideal.

ishtāpurta   Sacrificial rites (*ishta*) and acts of charity like the excavation of public wells (*purta*).

Ishwara   The Supreme Ruler, the Lord of Creation, God.

Itihāsa   History (often mixed with myths and legends).

Jagaddhātri   Name of God as the Divine Mother in a particular form.

japa   Repetition of a holy name or word-symbol of God in any form often accompanied by counting of beads,—a spiritual practice on the Path of Love.

jātyantara-parināma   Transformation of one genus or species into another.

jihvā   Tongue; the subtle organ of taste as well as of speech corresponding to the tongue. *See* indriya(s).

jiva   The soul; also, a living being.

jivanmukta   (*Lit.*, liberated while living) One who has reached the goal of liberation before death.

jivātman   The soul of an individual.

jnāna Knowledge, particularly knowledge of the eternal verities.

Jnāna-kānda The section of the Vedas dwelling mainly on the eternal verities, (mainly the Upanishads and certain portions of the *Brāhmanas*).

Jnāna-yoga The Path of Knowledge,—one of the four fundamental types of spiritual discipline.

Jnāna-yogi One going through the scheduled spiritual discipline of the Path of Knowledge.

jnanendriya(s) Subtle organs of knowledge corresponding to the outer instruments, *viz*, the eyes, ears, nose, tongue and skin. *See* indriya(s).

Jyotisha Astronomy; (also, Astrology).

Kāli Name of God as the Divine Mother in a particular form.

kalpa Brahmā's day and night. A periodic cycle of Creation and Dissolution.

kāma Lust; desire.

kāma-kānchana Lust and gold (possession), *i.e.*, greed.

karana Instrument (of knowledge and action); the subtle or psychic body as the instrument of knowledge and action.

kārana Cause; the unmanifested potential cause that, in due time, takes shape as the visible effect; the material cause of the universe in such a state during the period of Dissolution, *i.e.*, Cosmic Energy in a potential condition.

kārana-salila 'Primeval water'; the potential condition of the Cosmic Energy described figuratively as the water of an all-pervading sea. *See* ekārnava.

kārana-sharira The causal body (where the individual retires during sound sleep, the intellect, mind and sense-organs being reduced to an unmanifested potential condition); this is the proximate cover of the soul, known also as the sheath of bliss.

karma Action, deed, work; duty; ritualistic work.

Karma-kānda The section of the Vedas dwelling mainly on rituals.

karma-phala (*Lit.*, the fruit of an action) The consequence of a deed in the shape of pain or pleasure,—of three kinds, *viz.*, *prārabdha*, *samchita* and *kriyamāna*.

Karma-yoga The Path of Action; one of the four fundamental types of spiritual discipline.

Karma-yogi One going through the scheduled spiritual discipline of the Path of Action.

karmabhumi Land of action (this world is referred to as such).

Karmavāda The doctrine of *karma* upholding that each deed, good or bad, is inevitably followed by pleasure or pain as its sure effect.

karmendriya(s) Subtle organs of action corresponding to hands, feet, tongue and the external organs of evacuation and reproduction. *See* indriya(s).

kartā Doer; the subject of action.

kārya Effect (correlative of kārana); the physical body is described as *kārya* in contrast to the causal body (*kārana*).

kathaka One who narrates (particularly myths, legends and history).

kosha(s) (*Lit.*, sheath, scabbard) A sheath enclosing the soul. There are five such concentric sheaths or chambers, one above the other, *viz.*, the sheaths of bliss, intelligence, mind, vital energy and food or physical matter,—the soul residing within the innermost one, *viz.*, the sheath of bliss.

krama-mukti Gradual liberation after death through stages in the higher worlds.

Krishna An Incarnation of God as *Vishnu* (the Preserver); one of the chosen Ideals of the Vaishnavas.

kriyamāna (*Lit.*, what is being done) The effect of the deeds of the present life to be experienced in future. *See* karma-phala.

Kshātra-dharma Code of life and conduct of the warrior class.

Kshatriya A primary social group. *See* varna.

kshiti Earth. *See* bhuta(s).

Kurma (Tortoise) One of the Incarnations of God according to Hindu mythology.

lilā Sport; the cosmos looked upon as a Divine play.

Lilāmayi A connotative name of the Divine Mother to whom Creation and Dissolution are mere sports.

linga Sign; symbol; *also*, Shivalinga.

linga-sharira The subtle or psychic body (that becomes particularly active during the dream-state by creating a world of its own),—the three sheaths of intelligence, mind and vital energy constitute this body.

loka Any of the worlds inhabited by living beings.

madhura   The attitude of a devotee expressing amorous relationship with God, looking upon Him as the Beloved. *See* bhāva.

mahākāvya   An epic.

mahāpurusha   (*Lit.*, a great soul) A sage.

Mahad-brahman   *See* Hiranyagarbha.

mahimā   Glory; spiritual power.

manana   Cogitation, reflection—particularly on the eternal verities,—the second of the three steps on the Path of Knowledge.

manas   Mind.

mānasa pujā   Mental worship,—an item of ritualistic worship requiring the devotee to go mentally through the entire procedure of worship.

mānava dharma   The essential nature of man; religion of man.

manomaya kosha   The mental sheath. *See* kosha(s).

mantra   A sacred formula to be uttered in connection with rituals; also a mystic syllable, *i.e.*, a sacred word-symbol (of God in any particular form) to be repeated by devotees on the Path of Love.

Mārga   Path.

Matsya   (Fish) One of the Incarnations of God according to Hindu mythology.

Māyā   (Enchantment; illusion) According to a Vedānta school the mysterious Divine Power of Becoming through which God projects the illusory appearance of the cosmos; same as Avidyā and Avyakta.

Mitra   A Vedic deity.

mlechchha   A term of contempt implying a non-Hindu with outlandish habit and customs (cf. 'heathen' and 'kafir')

mukta purusha   A person liberated from all kinds of bondage.

mukti (moksha)   Liberation from all kinds of bondage; absolute freedom,—the goal of spiritual endeavour.

naimittika pralaya   Occasional Cosmic Dissolution (during *Hiranyagarbha's* sleep). *See* Pralaya.

Nārāyana   Another name of Vishnu. *See* Vishnu.

nāsikā   Nose; the subtle organ of smell corresponding to the outer instrument, the nose. *See* indriya(s).

nididhyāsana   Concentration on Self-knowledge,—the last of the three steps on the Path of Knowledge.

Nigama　A class of *Tāntrika* literature. *See* also Tantra(s).

Nirākāra　Formless.

Nirguna　Devoid of attributes.

nirvikalpa samādhi　A super-conscious state during which the aspirant realizes his absolute oneness with the Universal Spirit.

nishedha　Prohibition (enjoined by the Scriptures).

nitya karma　Rituals for everyday performance (obligatory during the first three stages of life).

nitya pralaya　Dissolution of everyday occurrence during an individual's sound sleep. *See* Pralaya.

Nivritti Mārga　The Path of Renunciation (of desires).

niyama　A preliminary course of moral discipline prescribed by Rāja-yoga. *See* Ashtānga-yoga.

Nrisimha　(*Lit.*, man-lion) One of the Incarnations of God according to Hindu mythology.

Nri-yajna　Service of human beings,—one of the five sacrificial rites enjoined on all householders.

nyāsa　A ritualistic process in *Tāntrika* worship intended to sanctify the physical body.

panchikarana　(*Lit.*, quintupling) According to the Vedānta school a particular process by which the five kinds of the elementary constituents of the universe are said to be compounded with one another to form grosser entities (that serve as units in the composition of the physical universe). *See* bhuta(s).

pāpa (pāpmā)　Sin; a wicked deed; evil.

Pāpa purusha　Evil personified.

para(ā)　Supreme.

parā bhakti　Supreme devotion; supreme love for God.

Parabrahma(n)　The Supreme Reality, the Absolute.

Parā Prakriti　The Higher Cosmic Energy through which God appears as individual souls.

pāramārthika　In an absolute sense (as opposed to vyāvahā-rika),—a Vedāntic word.

Paramātman　The Supreme Self, the Universal Spirit.

Parameshwara　The Supreme Lord of Creation, God.

parināma　Transformation.

Parināmavāda　The doctrine of transformation (of the school of conditioned Non-dualism) upholding that God actually transforms a portion of His Being into the universe.

Pārshada   A companion; according to Vaishnava literature an exalted spiritual personage accompanying an Incarnation of God.

Pārvati   An Incarnation of the Divine Mother.

pashwāchāra   (*Lit.*, conduct of brutes) A *Tāntrika* course of spiritual discipline for the least advanced aspirants.

pata   Picture.

Paurānika   Mythological.

Pitriloka   The world of the manes.

Pitri-yajna   Oblations for gratifying the manes,—one of the five sacrificial rites enjoined on all householders.

prabuddha   Awakened; conscious of the Ultimate Reality.

Prajāpati   A Hindu deity, also called *Virāt*.

Prājna   A name according to Vedānta philosophy of the individual in the causal state (as in sound sleep),—the Supreme Reality appears as such through the veil of an individual causal body.

prākrita Pralaya   Cosmic Dissolution at the end of *Hiranyagarbha's* span of life, when he becomes liberated. *See* Pralaya.

prakriti: Prakriti*   Causal state, nature: *Cosmic Energy, the Divine Power of Becoming.

Pralaya   (*Lit.*, complete merging) Dissolution (when the cosmos merges into (i) its unseen immediate cause, *viz.*, the unmanifested Cosmic Energy or (ii) in the ultimate substratum of Absolute Reality) of four kinds,—*nitya, naimittika, prākrita* and *ātyantika*: the first three of type (i) and the last of (ii).

prāna(s): Prāna*   Vital energy,—said to be of five kinds corresponding to five different kinds of physiological functions (hence used in plural). The five are called *prāna, apāna, samāna, udāna* and *vyāna*: *See* Hiranyagarbha.

prāna-pratishthā   A (*Tāntrika*) ritualistic process by which an image or symbol of God or any deity is said to be vitalized.

prānamaya kosha   The sheath of vital energy. *See* kosha(s).

prānāyāma   A kind of breathing exercise as a step towards concentration of mind. *See* Ashtānga-yoga. It has a place also in *Tāntrika* worship.

prārabdha   The portion of karma-phala that determines one's present life. *See* karma-phala.

Prasthānatraya   .Name of the trio of scriptural texts, *viz.*, the *Brahma Sutras*, the Upanishads and the *Gitā*.

pratika   A symbol representing God or a deity for facilitating worship and spiritual contemplation.

pratimā   An image representing God or a deity for facilitating worship and spiritual contemplation.

pratyāhāra   The process of detaching the subtle sense-organs from their corresponding outer instruments on the physical body. *See* Ashtānga-yoga.

Pravritti Mārga   The Path of Desire,—a preliminary course of spiritual discipline.

punya   A meritorious deed; virtue.

Purāna(s)   A class of popular scriptural texts in which spiritual teachings are imparted through a garb of myths and legends; mythology.

Purushottama   (*Lit.*, the Supreme Person) The Supreme Lord of the universe.

Putreshti yāga   A sacrificial rite performed with the object of getting a son.

Rāja-yoga   The Path of Concentration,—one of the four fundamental types of spiritual discipline.

rājarshi   (*Lit.*, sage-king) One who is a king and also a seer of spiritual truths.

rajas   One of the three aspects or component traits of Cosmic Energy,—the principle of dynamism in nature bringing about all changes,—through this is projected the relative appearance of the absolute as the universe (vital energy and the subtle organs of action have this in their make-up), —in individual nature predominance of this generates passions and restlessness.

rājasika   Energetic, ambitious and restless due to predominance of rajas in one's nature.

Rāma(chandra)   An Incarnation of God as *Vishnu* (the Preserver),—one of the chosen Ideals of the Vaishnavas; God (in a general sense).

rasa   Taste; the sensation of taste; also essence of enjoyment.

ripu   (*Lit.*, a foe) The six passions, *viz.*, lust, anger, greed, infatuation, conceit and jealousy.

rishi: Rishi-yajna Seer of God, sage: study of the Scriptures for gratifying the seers of God,—one of the five sacrificial rites enjoined on all householders.

rupa Form (in a general sense); colour as the object of perception through the organ of sight; the sensation of colour.

sādhaka An aspirant going through any course of spiritual discipline.

sādhanā Spiritual practice or endeavour.

Saguna Having attributes (as opposed to Nirguna).

Sākāra Having a form (as opposed to Nirākāra).

sakhya The attitude of a devotee expressing the relationship of a friend with God. *See* bhāva.

Sākshi-chaitanya Consciousness as witness of mental functions.

samādhi Concentration *par excellence*, trance, a super-conscious stage. *See* Ashtānga-yoga.

samashti An integrated whole of the same class of entity; *e.g.*, *samashti buddhi* (Cosmic Intelligence).

samatwam Equanimity under all conditions; equability of outlook (making no distinction between friend and foe, pain and pleasure, etc.).

samchita A portion of past *karma-phala* that lies stored up for experience in future births. *See* karma-phala.

samghāta Combination.

Samhitā(s) One of the two primary sections of each of the Vedas containing hymns and sacred formulae, the other being *Brāhmana*(s).

sampradāya Sect.

samsāra Life through repeated births and deaths; the world; worldly life.

samskāra(s) Subtle mental impressions (in which state previous experiences lie stored up in the mind).

samsriti Repeated passing (through births and deaths).

samyama Control (particularly of the mind and the senses); a technical name of the combination of the last three steps of spiritual discipline according to Rāja-yoga.

Sandhyā Vandanā A simple Vedic ritual to be performed daily by the members of the first three social groups during the first three stages of their life.

Sannyāsa Renunciation of social ties; the last stage of Hindu life, *viz.*, the stage of complete renunciation. *See* āshrama.

Sannyāsi   A monk, one who has embraced the life of complete renunciation, one belonging to the fourth stage of life, *viz.*, *Sannyāsa*.

Satchidānanda-sāgara   The ocean of Existence, Knowledge and Bliss,—a metaphorical expression suggesting the indescribable Absolute Reality.

sattwa   One of the three aspects or component traits of Cosmic Energy,—the principle of poise in nature,—through this things are revealed to consciousness (the intellect, mind and subtle organs of knowledge have this in their make-up), —in individual nature predominance of this generates purity, equanimity and the power of clear vision.

sāttwika   Having *sattwa* predominantly in one's nature and hence endowed with purity, equanimity and clear vision. *See* sattwa.

Saura   A Hindu sect worshipping God as *Surya*: a member of this sect; pertaining to this sect.

Shad-Darshana   The six systems of Hindu philosophy, *viz.*, (*Purva*) *Mimānsā*, *Nyāya*, *Vaisheshika*, *Yoga*, *Sāmkhya* and *Vedānta* (*Uttara Mimānsā*).

Shaiva   A Hindu sect worshipping God as *Shiva*; a member of this sect; pertaining to this sect.

Shaiva Āgama(s)   A class of scriptural texts of the Shaiva sect.

Shāka   A Hindu sect worshipping God as the Divine Mother; a member of this sect; pertaining to this sect.

shakti: Shakti*   Power: *general *Tāntrika* name of God as the Divine Mother, connoting the apparent dynamic aspect of the Eternal Being as the Supreme Power of Creation, Preservation and Destruction of the universe; the Divine Power of Becoming; Cosmic Energy.

Shālagrāma-shilā   A variety of rounded stone with certain marks on it, used as symbol of God as *Vishnu*.

shānta   The (unemotional) attitude of calmness of a devotee contemplating on the infinite glories of Personal God,— this attitude does not express any earthly relationship with Him. *See* bhāva.

sharira   Body.

Shāstra(s)   (*Lit.*, that which governs) The Scriptures (that govern Hindu life and conduct).

shabda   Sound; the sensation of sound.

Shiva   God in a particular form,—the chosen Ideal of the Shaiva sect. One of the Hindu Trinity representing God as the Destroyer. *See* Brahmā

Shivalinga   A symbol of God as *Shiva*, made of stone, metal or clay.

Shodashi   Name of God as the Divine Mother in a particular form.

shravana   The first of the three steps of spiritual discipline on the Path of knowledge, consists of hearing about the eternal verities from the spiritual guide and the Scriptures.

shreyas   Ultimate good, *i.e.*, perfection and eternal bliss.

shrotra   Ear; the subtle organ of hearing corresponding to the ears. *See* indriya(s).

Shruti   (*Lit.*, anything heard) Revealed knowledge,—the Vedas.

shubha   Good; (auspicious).

Shudra   A primary social group. *See* varna.

shunya   Void.

siddha   One who has succeeded in reaching the goal of liberation.

siddhi(s)   Occult powers.

Smriti(s)   (*Lit.*, anything remembered) Any Scripture other than the Vedas, specially one laying down social and domestic laws.

sparsha   Touch; the sensation of touch.

Sphota   The eternal sound according to a school (*Mimānsā*) of Hindu philosophy.

Srishti   (*Lit.*, projection) Creation.

Sthiti   Continued existence,—the state of the universe during the interval between Creation and Dissolution.

sthula   Gross; physical, as opposed to subtle (*sukshma*) and causal (*kārana*).

sukshma   Fine; subtle; belonging to a subtler order of existence than the physical.

Surya   (*Lit.*, the sun) A Hindu deity; God in a particular form as the chosen Ideal of one of the Hindu sects.

sushupti   Sound sleep.

Suta(s)   A class of people in ancient India serving as minstrels and chroniclers in royal courts.

sutra(s)   Aphorism; a terse saying, almost a suggestive formula, embodying a lesson (different subjects were epitomized by the Hindu writers through such pithy sayings).

Sutrātma   *See* Hiranyagarbha.

Swadhā   A Vedic word interpreted as the mysterious Divine Power of Becoming, *i.e.*, *Māyā* or *Avidyā*.

swadharma   The religion or code of duties of a Hindu according to his stage of life and station in society.

swādhyāya   Study of Scriptures.

Taijasa   A name used in Vedānta philosophy for an individual in the subtle state (as in dream),—when the Supreme Reality is veiled and coloured by an individual subtle body, It appears as *Taijasa*.

tamas   One of the aspects or component traits of Cosmic Energy,—the principle of inertia, ignorance and insentience in nature,—through this Reality is veiled (the physical universe has this in its make-up), in individual nature predominance of this generates lethargy and ignorance.

tāmasika   Lethargic and ignorant.

tanmātra(s)   (*Lit.*, that alone) the elementary constituents of the universe. *See* bhuta(s).

Tantra(s)   A class of scriptural texts (not derived directly from the Vedas) presenting God as the Divine Mother and prescribing elaborate and often esoteric rituals,—of two varieties, *Āgama* and *Nigama*; (some of the Shaiva and Vaishnava scriptural texts are also referred to as Tantras).

Tāntrika   A Hindu sect worshipping God as the Divine Mother; a member of this sect; pertaining to Tantra (Tāntric).

Tārā   Name of God as the Divine Mother in a particular form.

tarpana   Libation of water for gratifying the manes.

tejas   Same as agni. *See* bhuta(s).

Trigunamayi   A connotative name of God as the Divine Mother suggesting that She possesses the three phases of Energy, *viz.*, *sattwa*, *rajas* and *tamas*.

Trignunātmikā   Characterized by three traits, *viz.*, *sattwa*, *rajas* and *tamas*,—an attribute of the Cosmic Energy or the Divine Power of Becoming (*Māyā*, *Avidyā*, *Avyakta*, *Prakriti*).

twak   Skin; the subtle organ of touch corresponding to the skin. *See* indriya(s).

upādhi   A superimposed thing or attribute that veils and gives a coloured view of the distinct substance beneath it; limiting adjunct; a technical term used in Vedānta philosophy for any superimposition that gives a limited view of the Absolute and makes it appear as the Relative.

Upāgama(s) Subsidiary scriptural texts connected with a Shaiva *Āgama*. *See* Shaiva Āgama(s).

Upanishad(s) The well-known Hindu Scriptures included in the Vedas dwelling mainly on the eternal verities of life and existence.

upāsanā (*Lit.*, sitting near) Worship or contemplation of God or a deity.

vāda Doctrine.

vaidhi (*Lit.*, according to a set code of injunctions) Formalistic.

vaidhi bhakti Formalistic devotion (at the initial stage on the Path of Love), practice of devotion through a set code of rituals as a preparatory course for developing intense love for God.

Vaishnava A Hindu sect worshipping God as *Vishnu*; a member of this sect; pertaining to this sect.

Vaishya A primary social group. *See* varna.

Vāmana (*Lit.*, a dwarf) One of the Incarnations of God according to Hindu mythology.

Vānaprastha The third stage of Hindu life, *viz.*, the stage of retirement and contemplation. *See* āshrama.

Varāha (Boar) One of the Incarnations of God according to Hindu mythology.

varna Any of the four primary social groups according to qualifications and vocations, *viz.*, Brāhmana (priests, teachers and law-makers), Kshatriya (warriors and kings), Vaishya (traders, bankers, industrialists and farmers) and Shudra (labourers).

varnāshrama Related to the four primary social groups and the four stages of Hindu life.

Varuna A Hindu deity.

vātsalya The attitude of a devotee expressing parental relationship with God, looking upon Him as a child. *See* bhāva.

vāyu: Vāyu* Air. *See* bhuta(s): A Hindu deity.

vedanā Feeling, sensation; (pain).

Vedānta (*Lit.*, the end of the Vedas) The Upanishads; the school of Hindu thought (based primarily on the Upanishads) upholding the doctrine of either pure Non-dualism or conditioned Non-dualism (the original text of this school is *Vedānta Darshana* or *Uttara Mimānsā* or the *Brahma Sutras* compiled by the sage Vyāsa); pertaning to this school of thought.

vibhuti(s)   Supernormal power.

videha-mukti   Liberation at the end of the present life.

vidhi   Injunction (enjoined by the Scriptures).

vijnānamaya kosha   The sheath of intelligence. *See* kosha(s).

vikshepa shakti   One of the aspects or component powers of Nescience functioning as the apparent distorter of Reality.

virāchāra   (*Lit.*, conduct of heroic souls) A *Tāntrika* course of spiritual discipline for the heroic types of devotees.

Virāt   A Vedic deity; a cosmic being with the entire physical universe as his body.

vishaya   Object of perception (related to an organ of knowledge).

Vishishtādvaita-vāda   The doctrine of conditioned Non-dualism (of a Vedānta school upholding that the One actually becomes many).

Vishnu   God as the Preserver,—one of the Hindu Trinity also called *Nārāyana*. (Rāma and Krishna are regarded as Incarnations of *Vishnu*). The chosen Ideal of the Vaishnavas in any of these forms.

Vishwa   A name used in Vedānta philosophy for an individual in the gross state (as during the waking period),—when the Supreme Reality is veiled and coloured by an individual physical body, It appears as *Vishwa*; (universe).

vivarta   Illusory appearance (a doctrine of the Non-dualistic school of Vedānta philosophy explaining creation as an illusory appearance of the Absolute, is known as *Vivarta-vāda*).

viveka   Discrimination.

vritti   Condition; mode; modification; function.

vyashti   Individual (as opposed to samashti).

vyāvahārika   In an apparent and relative sense, as opposed to pāramārthika (a technical word of Vedānta philosophy).

yajna (yāga)   Sacrificial rite.

yama   A preliminary course of moral discipline prescribed by Rāja-yoga. *See* Ashtānga-yoga.

yavana   (*Lit.*, an Ionian, a Greek) A term of contempt implying a non-Hindu with outlandish habit and customs (cf. 'heathen' and 'kafir').

yoga   (*Lit.*, union) Union with God; any course of spiritual discipline that makes for such union; concentration of mind; Rāja-yoga; unruffled state of mind under all conditions.

Yogamāyā   A *Paurānika* name of the mysterious Divine Power of Becoming.

yogi   One who strives earnestly for union with God; an aspirant going through any course of spiritual discipline; one going particularly through the scheduled course of Rāja-yoga; a spiritually advanced person with a perfectly unruffled mind under all conditions.

INDEX